FURTHER

Also by Michael Hutchinson

The Hour: Sporting Immortality the Hard Way

Faster: The Obsession, Science and Luck Behind the World's Fastest Cyclists

Re:Cyclists: 200 Years on Two Wheels

MICHAEL HUTCHINSON

FURTHER

SEEKING THE DISTANT LIMITS OF CYCLING ENDURANCE

ALLEN&UNWIN

First published in hardback in Great Britain in 2025 by
Allen & Unwin, an imprint of Atlantic Books Ltd.

Copyright © Michael Hutchinson, 2025

The moral right of Michael Hutchinson to be identified as the
author of this work has been asserted by him in accordance
with the Copyright, Designs and Patents Act of 1988.

All rights reserved. No part of this publication may be reproduced, stored in a retrieval system, or transmitted in any form or by any means, electronic, mechanical, photocopying, recording, or otherwise, without the prior permission of both the copyright owner and the above publisher of this book.

No part of this book may be used in any manner in the learning, training or development of generative artificial intelligence technologies (including but not limited to machine learning models and large language models (LLMs)), whether by data scraping, data mining or use in any way to create or form a part of data sets or in any other way.

Every effort has been made to trace or contact all copyright holders. The publishers will be pleased to make good any omissions or rectify any mistakes brought to their attention at the earliest opportunity.

1 3 5 7 9 8 6 4 2

A CIP catalogue record for this book is available from the British Library.

Hardback ISBN: 978 1 80546 045 9
Trade Paperback ISBN: 978 1 80546 046 6
E-book ISBN: 978 1 80546 047 3

Typeset by Tetragon, London
Printed and bound by CPI (UK) Ltd, Croydon CR0 4YY

Atlantic Books
An imprint of Atlantic Books Ltd
Ormond House
26–27 Boswell Street
London
WC1N 3JZ

www.atlantic-books.co.uk

Product safety EU representative: Authorised Rep Compliance Ltd., Ground Floor, 71 Lower Baggot Street, Dublin, D02 P593, Ireland. www.arccompliance.com

Contents

1	The Half-day from Hell	1
2	The Best You Can Be Right Now	23
3	The Never-Exceed Speed	61
4	Very Long Rides Don't Make You Fast, They Just Make You Tired	93
5	14,000 Calories a Day	119
6	Reinventing the Bike Race and the Rise of the Amateurs	147
7	Fifteen Minutes, the Perfect Night's Sleep	167
8	A Perfect Equilibrium of Discomfort	187
9	A 3 a.m. Lesson in Trust	213
10	The Hutch Moment	237

Acknowledgements	253
Index	255

1

The Half-day from Hell

Cycling has a self-satisfied saying: 'The worst day on a bike is better than the best day at work.' To which I say, maybe you've just never had a properly bad day on a bike?

I am going to start out by telling you about one of the worst days of not just my bike-riding career, but my life. It failed to be the absolute worst only because it was something I did entirely of my own free will. It wasn't a bereavement, or a shipwreck, or a house fire. It was only a bike race, one where no one got hurt, and so decency demands I keep a sense of perspective, however unwillingly.

It was the British National 12 Hour Time Trial Championship, all the way back in 2000, in Bedfordshire in England. These events, based on how far you can ride in a set time, on your own and with no chance to draft behind anyone else, are very traditional and rather old-fashioned. You can trace them back to the Victorian era just by reading the little plaques on the trophies. This race, which started near Biggleswade, was based on a course that had been in use for over 100 years, and the whole event felt like an antique.

There was a level crossing, and beside it sat an octogenarian in a deckchair with a stopwatch and a clipboard, timing how long you were stopped for if the barriers were down. It was that sort of thing.

There were about 100 of us who set out at dawn on a windy morning in early September to ride a complicated series of laps and out-and-backs up and down various main roads around Bedfordshire and Cambridgeshire, finishing on a shorter six-mile circuit which we'd lap for the final couple of hours to allow the timekeepers to calculate an exact distance.

I had only decided to do the race 10 days before it happened, because I was having a racing season where everything I had touched turned to gold. I'd won almost every event I'd entered, including three other National titles, one of them by the biggest margin seen in three decades. By September I believed, in essence, that I could do no wrong. I was wrong about that. I had very little idea what I was doing. I paced the race badly. My nutrition was all over the place. I hadn't really thought through how I might cope when the going got hard. What I did have was proper motivation – I really, really wanted to win the event, because if I could, I'd have won a series of British championships across an unprecedented range of distances, from 10 miles to 12 hours, and that was something I very much liked the idea of having on my CV. In sport as in life, incompetence and determination is a fabulous combination if you want to dig yourself deep into a very unhappy place.

By the five-hour mark I'd started crying. I kept crying till the end. The first hour or two had been all right. But I'd started out too hard, and I'd tried to eat too much as I went, which quickly made me sick. By five hours in I was leading the race, but I was a mess. I don't remember anything actually hurting in an acute way, other than my backside and my feet, which wasn't anything that I couldn't have dealt with. What I was sinking under was a deep, rootless fatigue. It was dizziness, nausea, blurred vision. It was a despair so vast it didn't really have a location. Just keeping going, against the overwhelming scale of the seven hours that were left to go, was almost more than I could do. Every turn of the pedals felt like an individual challenge.

I cried for seven hours, out of disappointment with myself and my inexperience, and out of the loneliness that came from only seeing my support crew for a fleeting, on-the-fly hand up of a bottle and some food once an hour. When someone asked me afterwards if I'd thought about stopping, I said yes. When he asked how often, I said just once, but the thought had lasted for seven hours.

I was sick, frequently. But I also knew I had to keep the energy coming in, so there were instances when I took a mouthful of energy drink, vomited it back up instantly, took another mouthful and repeated the process with a sort of resignation. I think that if you'd watched me doing it, you would have concluded that it was what I was trying to do. Compared to the way I felt about everything else, it wasn't a big deal. In a similar scenario in a similar race, a friend once smeared energy gel over his forearms because he had become convinced he could absorb carbohydrate through his skin like a mollusc. He was a normal, intelligent person who would not have believed this under any other circumstances. He finished the race pebble-dashed with flies that had never experienced a sugar bonanza like it.

I kept going by working from landmark to landmark. 'Just ride to the junction.' 'Just ride to that sign in the distance.' 'Ride to the level crossing, and with a bit of luck it will be down and you can stop and have a chat with the guy in the deckchair.' The crossing was never down, and just as well. When that approach got too hard, instead of just riding to the junction, I promised myself that if I rode to the junction I could give up when I got there. I must have made this deal 100 times, but never took myself up on it. Every time stopping just seemed like too big a thing to do, too final, too weak. I think I kept racing because I lacked the breadth of imagination to stop – although in some ways that's just how bike racing works.

In the end I did actually take the championship title. I covered 293 miles, to take the win by just 2.5 miles, or around five minutes. I was not in good shape. A magazine report noted that I was still visibly shaking an hour after I'd finished. A friend who was a nurse and at the race as a spectator went to fetch another friend who was a doctor. She was anxious that I was about to go into cardiac arrest because I'd gone grey. ('And not a good grey, Michael,' she later told me. 'Even your hair seemed to have gone grey. Apart from the bloodshot eyes, you looked as if you were in black and white.')

Another friend later told me that my experience had reminded him of a 12-hour he'd ridden in the 1980s, on the hottest day of the summer. 'When my support crew caught up with me just after the finish, I was in such a state that they thought I was going to die,' he said. 'When my wife got there, she thought I was going to die. When the paramedics got there, they thought I was going to die.' I wasn't quite that bad, but it felt like it.

At the time I didn't think the result was worth it – I remember waiting for the prize-giving and thinking I might never be quite the same again. Now I'd say it was, but only because when the 'worst day on a bike' discussion comes around, and it regularly does, I normally win.

It was not a good race, and despite the result I didn't take much pride in it. I was almost embarrassed – not by the result, but by the state I reduced myself to. It didn't feel very professional. Also, I didn't really know quite what to make of the experience. I was a good bike rider, especially a good time trial rider. That season I'd won championship races over 10, 50 and 100 miles, and finished second in the 25-mile event. None of those had been especially traumatic – they'd all been well-executed, straightforward races. They hadn't been easy, but nor had they been especially difficult. They had gone according to plan. I'd been in control, of both the race and myself, which was how I liked it. At no point in any of them, even when they were at their hardest, would I have voluntarily stopped. I enjoyed riding them, because I was riding at my best. In contrast, I did not much like the drawn-out, vomity misery of the 12-hour, where despite the result I felt like the victim rather than the victor.

The final insult was that there are two potential physical responses to that sort of ride. One is that a week or two later you get a spike in fitness, and a few weeks of all-conquering race form. The other is that it takes weeks of feeling lousy for your condition to recover to something you'd describe as 'bad' rather than simply 'this person is not an athlete', and you probably don't even manage that before the end of the season. Guess which I got.

I was not good at this sort of long race, I decided. It would make sense. My shorter distance career was founded on a huge aerobic system. I had, essentially, the heart and lungs of a horse, and over anything up to four or five hours it was very effective. I'd like to say up front that while this is a sort of a brag, I didn't do very much to deserve this. It's largely genetic luck. My perception at the time, right or wrong, was that if you wanted to race over what I had come to regard as stupidly long distances, you needed a different toolkit, one that leaned more heavily on things like efficiency and the proportion of your maximum effort you could sustain over time. That, and the ability to eat and drink a lot while riding a bike without getting into the territory that is delicately referred to in the literature as 'gastrointestinal distress'. I hadn't seemed especially blessed in that area either. I decided the whole thing was not my forte and went back to the things I was good at.

*

What I was good at was short to middle distance time trial riding. Very simple races against the clock, at distances that traditionally consisted of 10, 25, 50 and 100 miles. Time trial riding is part of elite international cycling, but in something of a subsidiary role. It's part of most stage races. There's the World Championships and the various regional and national championships, but very few other stand-alone international time trial races. There's no real space at that level of pro cycling for someone who rides almost nothing but time trials. In the UK, however, for historical reasons that date back almost to the invention of cycle racing, time trialling as an end in itself has always been a bigger deal. Until the 1950s, it was almost all there was, because mass-start road racing was banned. It has continued on as a slightly eccentric discipline, like a cross between Morris dancing and fell running.

That's how I was able to spend several years as a professional cyclist, riding very largely short time trials. My physiology and skill set were very well adapted to the sort of high-powered, moderate length (up to four hours) efforts needed. I was nerdy enough to really enjoy working on things like aerodynamics, and savvy enough to find sponsors and ensure I kept my profile nice and high. The happy upshot was that I won everything there was to win in the UK multiple times, with the exception of the shortest race, the hill-climb championships (races over just a couple of minutes up a very steep hill, dominated by light riders with physiology tending towards the sprint) and the longest race, the 24-hour. In total I won almost 60 national titles in Britain, another three in Ireland, and broke all the UK records up to 100 miles. UK time trialling is a small world, but for a while at least, I was its apex predator.*

---

* I've got dual Irish-British nationality, and did my international racing for Ireland. But the UK events are run on an all-comers basis.

I largely stuck to my resolution to avoid the longer time trials of anything over 100 miles. (Even 100 miles at the speed I used to do it took less than three and a half hours, which is hardly a long ride in terms of duration.) I rode some longer mass-start road races, but they're a different animal because the effort level varies much more, so there's a bit of recovery built in. But I did have occasional lapses. I rode a 12-hour again three years after the first debacle, as I attempted to rescue the 2003 season, the least successful of my career, from total anonymity. I changed a few elements from the first misfire, but not enough, and not with sufficient understanding of the problems from the previous ride. The upshot was that the second race was every bit as bad as the first one, and this time it wasn't even underpinned by fundamentally good fitness. I had a similar day out without even much of a result to show for it, and it was a very dispiriting way to make a bad year worse. For the second time in three years I promised myself that it was not something I was going to put myself through again.

*

In the years that elapsed between that race and the present day, cycling changed a lot. From a sport where interest was focused almost exclusively on professional UCI racing and the men's World Tour (and its predecessor the ProTour), it became broader. Non-World Tour racing, like gravel events, became hugely popular, precisely because it had an anarchic spirit that was almost the opposite of the very exclusive, very expensive road pro scene. The sponsors and coaches of serious riders increasingly allowed, then encouraged, their riders to chop and change between road, track, gravel and mountain biking.

And there have been some long rides in this new mix, even among the elite pros, and sometimes with interesting results. In the 2021 Tour de France the EF Education–Nippo team's greatest success was way off to one side of the normal race. It was Australian team member Lachlan Morton riding the entire route of the Tour on his own, with no support, a few days ahead of the actual event. He fended for himself, slept where he could, ate in cafés and fixed his own problems. He even rode all the transfers that the race itself was going to do by bus or train or air so that he covered 5,500 km compared to the mere 3,400 km of the Tour. He raised £360,000 for the World Bicycle Relief charity, created a social media sensation and generated a much higher profile than anything his teammates were doing at the actual race. Riders, teams and sponsors notice things like that. Morton followed it up with a ride that circumnavigated Australia in 2024, covering 14,200 km in 30 days, with a similar fan following.

In terms of races and records rather than challenges, the last decade or so has seen several new ultra races like the Transcontinental Race, which crosses the continent of Europe, and the Race Around Ireland. In the UK, there have been more attempts on the long distance place-to-place records (London to Liverpool, Edinburgh to London, Land's End to John O'Groats, that sort of thing) in the last five or six years than there have been in the previous couple of decades. At the really ultra end of the scale there have been numerous attempts on the Round the World record, and even the record for the highest recorded mileage in a calendar year, a record that had been undisturbed since it was parked at 75,065 miles by Tommy Godwin of the UK in the early months of World War Two. As of 2017 it stands at a scarcely believable 86,573 miles by Amanda Coker from the US. I'll save you the maths – that's 237 miles a day.

Even among random bike-riding friends who just ride at the weekend for fun, there's an urge to undertake challenges like Everesting (riding up and down the same hill until you clock up an Everest's worth of climbing – it takes all day) or covering every single road in a certain radius of home. I could go on, but in short, things are getting long. People who once dreamed of going fast increasingly dream of going far.

*

I retired from serious racing in 2014. I did a few local club events, I went on a few cycling holidays as a minor celeb. And I started a cycling podcast, because there seemed to be a remarkable shortage of them. I made one show about ultra racing. Twelve hours would be on the short side for an ultra race; I ended up interviewing riders who'd ridden events like the Race Across America and the Transcontinental Race, both of which take about a week for the winners.

It was fascinating to me. My own racing, and even the other 'normal' races I'd been involved with as a coach or a consultant, demanded what seemed like a fairly narrow, well-refined set of skills and abilities. So hearing about how you deal with hallucinations, how you find a safe place to sleep if you're overcome with sleepiness at 1 a.m. in Albania, or how you buy 10,000 calories-worth of food in an unfamiliar supermarket, do it in eight minutes flat from saddle and back to saddle, and then eat it while riding an Alpine pass was a whole new perspective.

I took to dot-watching ultra races. That's the live spectator experience, which consists of watching a dot representing a rider, on a website map, creeping pixel-by-pixel across a continent. You can double-screen the map with a Google Street View image to see what the dot is looking at, what the dot is dealing with, and if the race doesn't have a pre-determined route, maybe try to guess where the dot will go next. Then you try to work out if the slower dots are going to catch your dot, or if your dot is going to catch the dots in front. If the dot stops moving, you can try to decide if it's asleep or having an existential crisis. On the screen it all happens at the speed of tectonic plates moving. And it's utterly captivating. The sheer lack of excitement and the minimal amount of information in front of you only add to your investment.

Unsurprisingly, all of this started to get inside my head. One of the great pleasures of cycling is that there are so many different ways to do it, from track sprinting to riding across North America, and that someone who does one of these things can instantly understand quite a lot about the other. I started thinking about riding all day and all night, just how it would feel tapping out a nice easy pace where the challenge was mainly about looking after yourself and trying to balance everything, things like effort, eating and riding position, finding an efficient steady state and then just doing it and doing it until either you reached the other ocean or something on or in you broke.

There was something else that I have not yet confessed to. I've told you about two very terrible 12-hour rides. After each of them I swore I'd never do another. So it's in line with the recidivist nature of my personality that there was actually a third, a return to the National Championships in 2005. This time it was in north Lincolnshire.

The third 12-hour was done for motives that lacked purity. I was offered money. I was riding for a sponsor that wanted to target all the National Championships up to the 12-hour, and I accepted the terms of the deal. Since the 12-hour Champs was late in the season that year, I was perhaps hoping that the team boss would somehow forget about it. He did not. So I started working out how to race a 12-hour in a way that was designed mainly to minimize the misery while still actually riding for 12 hours.

I got together with my coach, Jamie Pringle, and dismantled the event, trying to work out what it would take to do it well from a starting point in the actual physiology. We paid as little attention as possible to the conventional wisdom, which was that since you were inevitably going to fall apart around four or five hours in, you'd better set out very fast indeed so you could get some miles in the bank before you saw Jesus by the A-road. Instead, we did some science on how to manage long races. I don't imagine we were the first to do this, and we certainly didn't do any original research, but I didn't know of anyone in whose footsteps we were directly following.

THE HALF-DAY FROM HELL

In the lab, we worked out an accurate figure for how hard I could ride while my digestive system could keep up with supplying the fuel. Since the way you burn fuel during exercise changes over the length of a long ride, the main experimental protocol involved eight hours of more or less non-stop riding, and we did it twice. I did not miss the irony of trying to make a 12-hour ride easier by doing 16 hours of experimenting. But the upshot was that we worked out, with a high degree of confidence, exactly how hard I could ride, and exactly what I was going to eat and drink while I did it. I can't remember the precise numbers, but the riding power we came up with was around 270 watts and the carbohydrate intake was 75 grams an hour. (For some context, 270 watts is still more than the majority of riders can sustain for 20 minutes, and 75 g of carbohydrate is (or at least was) a fairly universal number, as we'll see later on.)

Then I just went to the race and rode at that exact, to me quite relaxed, pace from the start. Bear in mind that in those days I could ride 100 miles at around 350 watts, and in my previous 12-hours I probably didn't really ride all that much more slowly for the first part of the race. This time, after four hours I was modestly placed in the race, well behind the leader, and apparently out of it. Back at the race headquarters people were wondering aloud what was wrong with me. But we'd got our sums right. I trundled along all day, never wavering from the same speed, never in difficulty. The 75 g of carbohydrate an hour was perfectly doable – it was not a stressful target and because my body was never stretched to breaking point my gut worked perfectly happily throughout. Everything was under control;

I was a stable system, just like I would have been in a short race.

The worst I could say of it is that occasionally it was a little nerve-wracking, especially in the early stages. It felt so slow, and I kept getting time checks on other riders that were exactly as I expected, but alarming all the same. But as the hours passed, the entertainment offered by most of the other competitors imploding, exploding or striving to manage both at once more than made up for it. I cruised through the chaos and the broken riders, feeling almost more like a spectator than someone supposedly suffering alongside them. I rode my last hour faster than my first just because I could. I won comfortably, in every sense. My finish came about 10 miles from the race headquarters, and rather than get in the team car for the return trip I rode back just to finish the day with a flourish. I won the 12-hour Championships for a second time, and this time by 9 miles, or about 25 minutes. The total distance was modest – 286 miles – because race day coincided with a summer storm that reduced several riders to walking on one headwind section. All the same, I remember, embarrassingly, greeting my support team after the finish with a roar of, 'Just how great was I?' 'Thank you very much for your help,' would have been more appropriate, but it was clear that I'd finished that race in a very different condition from the previous attempts.

It was a fascinating contrast with the earlier efforts. It was both much more effective and much easier to do. It was odd to know that however straightforward it might have felt, pushing any harder would almost certainly have brought about a repeat of the previous Armageddons. It wasn't like an intense, short distance race with power numbers well over 400 watts and a heart rate hitting the limit at 185 bpm. With those, years of experience meant I could almost physically feel the edge between what I could do and what I couldn't. On a long event, the equivalent edge was in a totally different place, determined by different things, and you had to find it a different way. It had been one of the most significant learning experiences I'd had in the sport.

Still, it wasn't something I went back to. That was 2005. I was a pro rider for almost another decade, and never again raced a time trial longer than 100 miles. The teams and sponsors I spent the latter part of my career riding for weren't interested. I wasn't unhappy about this. I wouldn't have described the 12-hour as an event mastered. Certainly I'd taken a scientific approach, narrowed down a lot of the variables, and I'd ended up with what felt like a well-deserved outcome. But it was clear that over that sort of event it was never simple. There were too many experienced 12-hour riders who still suffered regular disasters. Even if their pacing wasn't as optimal as I now reckoned it could be, at least they were repeating the same process every time, so if the event was going to play fair with them they ought to have at least got the same sub-optimal result in a repeatable manner. It would be a bit cocky to decide I'd cracked it once and for always on the basis of a single ride. But I'll admit that a certain curiosity remained.

*

In my years in cycling, as a rider and as a coach, I've become very familiar indeed with the world of the short and fast. I've seen a lot of it, I know most of how it works. For me the long races I started dot-watching at and talking to riders about are familiar and foreign at the same time. It's the same sport, the same equipment, and the same basic physics and physiology, but turned to a different end. It offers the constant surprise of finding that what I thought I knew is only half right. What happens to your body in an hour's race isn't all that different to what happens in four hours. At a fundamental level, you do it the same way with some minor tuning for pace. But when you get to eight, 12 or 24 hours, or a week, or a month, things change. They don't change in a way that I can't understand, but often they change in a way I wouldn't necessarily have expected. It's a chance to get a whole new cycling education.

As I've started digging into all of this, trying to figure out the races and looking at some of the science, the openness of the ultra racing community has surprised me. I wouldn't necessarily describe the world of elite pro racing as deeply secretive. But ultra racing has a different-feeling enthusiasm. If you even vaguely suggest you're curious about it to someone, almost invariably they will then do everything they can to encourage you, short of paying your entry fee to an event. They will tell stories that make you want to be involved, give you advice, lend you equipment, even offer to come to a race and help. It almost made me suspicious – have they taken a disastrous wrong turn in their lives that they feel they can at the very least dilute by getting you to take it too?

THE HALF-DAY FROM HELL

Certainly I very quickly found myself looking back and reminiscing about my 12-hour rides, especially that last one, because it was really the only reference point I had in all of this. I'd love to say that if someone told me about winning the Race Across America, I resisted the urge to tell them in return about triumphantly riding around the Scunthorpe area for half a day, but you always feel like you need to bring something to the conversation and it was all I had.

And after a while, it seemed like the most natural thing in the world to want to go back and have another go, at that, or maybe even something a bit harder, a bit longer. There is a collective, joyous insanity to ultra racing that has an infectious quality, and it felt almost rational to want to know just how far I could go, how much I could ask of myself. And that is how I realized, in early 2023, that I didn't just want to know more about long bike races, I wanted to ride one.

The problem with 'I'm going to ride an ultra race' as a plan was that ultra racing was a side of the sport that I didn't really know all that much about. It's hard to dabble in ultra – it's like half-learning to fly. I didn't know if I'd be any good at long races. I didn't know what sort of event I should set out to attempt, from the perspectives of practicality, physiology, psychology, or even cost. I didn't know how to prepare, I didn't even really know who to ask for advice. If I had run into you at a club Christmas dinner and told you I was going to do an ultra race, I would not be able to answer a single one of the many questions you might ask in reply, except maybe 'why?' And even then, I wouldn't have wanted you to tug too hard on that.

The longer events I'd already done didn't really help very much. I only got to the 12-hour races because of a historical UK curiosity called the British Best All-Rounder competition, which started off in 1930 as an ingenious attempt to have a national championship event that you could do without having to travel anywhere. Instead, the championship was decided by taking everyone's fastest rides over 50 and 100 miles, and 12 hours, and working out the average speed in each race. Then, using a three-foot-long slide rule, they calculated an average of the averages, down to a thousandth of a mile per hour. This produced a number that, while not statistically representative of anything very concrete, allowed you to declare a winner.

For the next 60 or 70 years, this was British time trialling's biggest prize. That despite numerous oddities, like the fact you could have a top 10 for the year, none of whom had at any point raced each other. Or that the whole show could be turned upside down by a really nice day's racing weather at one particular event that produced a very fast set of times. Or that a tardily issued result sheet could leave a rider desperately scanning magazines and making phone calls to investigate whether they'd won a national title or not.

If we ignore that for a moment, it is noteworthy that the distances chosen as most appropriate for deciding an all-round rider were a 50-mile sprint, a 100-mile middle distance effort and a 12-hour marathon. In 1930, even the shortest of those was going to take comfortably over two hours to do. There were plenty of midfielders who were going to be doing three-, six- and 12-hour races. To be clear, this was a competition for amateurs and club riders. It wasn't meant to be easy, but nor was it intended to be an extreme challenge. It was a hangover from a Victorian era where a wagering culture had pushed events towards longer and longer feats of endurance.

But we'll come back to that later. For the moment, what matters is that in the early twenty-first century, you could be a bike racer with a distinct bent towards short distance races, yet find that riding a decent 50-mile race would lead to riding a 100-mile race and before you knew where you were, you'd be lining up for a 12-hour without really ever having had a chance to stop and think about it or work out how to ride it. A 12-hour was sufficiently mainstream that it was something your team would expect you to do.

But this time around, in 2023 and long retired as a pro, I was a volunteer. I could do whatever I liked, which made it much harder to pick a target since I wasn't being railroaded into it. So did I want to do a race? Attempt a record? Did I want to do a supported event, where a team follows you all the way, or an unsupported one where you look after yourself, buying food and drink as you go and sleeping as best you can? Did I want to ride for 12 hours again, or ride for two weeks?

In the end, the decision-making algorithm was about logistics and money. Ultra racing is neither simple to do nor cheap. I narrowed it down to two events, one a supported 500-mile race run by a commercial race promoter. The other was the British National 24 Hour Time Trial Championship – the big brother of the 12 Hour. The 500-miler came with an entry fee of around £1,200 and demanded two support vehicles and a crew of at least four. I could line up at the 24-hour for £40, the event was in Shropshire and the crew was optional. I didn't really see why I should pay over the odds for my misery, so the 24-hour it was.

It was also a smaller leap. If I set out on a week-long event, especially as a first venture, it was going to be a question of logistics rather than cycling. I wanted to do something that I felt I could approach as a race rather than a project. I'd spent a long time racing bikes, and at the very least I wanted to be able to bring some of that with me.

So the first thing I did was go and visit a friend called Mike Broadwith. I've raced against Mike for years, and over the shorter distances I am pleased to report that I'd never had any trouble beating him. He had, however, moved up in distance since then, and on to considerable glory. He'd won the 24-hour Championships three times, with a best distance of 537 miles in 2015. Also, even more impressive, he was the holder of the Land's End to John O'Groats record, 844 miles covered in an utterly terrifying 43 hours, 25 minutes and 13 seconds. That's an average speed of 19.4 mph (31.1 kph). He and I went for a ride from his home in Hertfordshire on a spring morning, and as we rode we talked about long bike rides.

I went looking for advice, and got a lot more. Mike's enthusiasm for the idea of me riding a 24 was such that he offered to run the show for me. Sitting outside a local café, he offered to set up the support team, work out a pacing plan, and come and be my crew chief. He was happy to provide a sort of ultra riding helpdesk. It meant I'd got advice on approaching the event that was pretty much definitive.

On the downside it meant that quite a lot of very high-quality excuses went out the window before I'd even entered the race. But that was something I was just going to have to live with.

2

The Best You Can Be Right Now

When I decided to ride a 24-hour time trial, almost every other rider I mentioned it to said something along the lines of, 'Wow. That's going to be horrendous. That's going to be the worst thing you've ever done – it'll just be agony and misery combined. Why would you want to do that to yourself, what's wrong with you?'

Eventually I got so exasperated with this that when a former teammate said, 'That's just the worst thing I can imagine doing,' I snapped, 'Shut up. I'm looking forward to it. I want to do it, I'm going to do it, and you're not going to spoil it for me.' He did not seem reassured about my mental stability.

So maybe the psychological issues around very long races begin way back at the point where you decide you want to do one in the first place. No one thinks you're crazy if you want to ride a 10-mile time trial, yet approached with enough verve, one of those can make your vision go black and white, so it's not exactly eating Easter eggs and playing with kittens. Threaten to ride something long, though, and literally everyone who's not also a rider of long races thinks you've lost it.

Having said all of that, the misery and suffering is an image that ultra riders often play up. It's rare for an ultra rider's account of a race not to include some instances of sustained unhappiness. Where a short distance racer's distinguishing characteristics are about speed and power, an ultra rider's are about overcoming. The key narrative twist in the story of winning an Olympic medal or even a Tour de France often happens weeks or months or years before the event – it might be a training session, a moment of psychological inspiration, even a childhood trauma of some sort. It's rarely mid-race. In ultra racing, that's almost always where it is. If winning the Olympic team pursuit is 95% training and 5% racing, winning an ultra race is, if not quite the inverse, at least 75% racing.

When my friend and advisor Mike Broadwith set his Land's End to John O'Groats record (usually known simply as the End-to-End) in 2018, probably the moment the story turns on was just north of Perth, with 233 of the 840 miles left to go. (A previous record holder, John Woodburn, had once said, 'Any fool can get to Perth,' which tells you something about the way an ultra race's point of balance is far from its centre. Since it's a well-known comment, it also, of course, introduces a certain psychological aura around Perth – there is literally a Perth state of mind.)

Broadwith had started to struggle to hold his head up – this is a classic physical complaint in events like the

End-to-End, Race Across America, even shorter things like the 24-hour, anything that tends towards an aerodynamic riding position. It was cold, it was raining hard. 'I started to not be able to see how this was going to work,' he said. 'I was having real problems looking up to see the road ahead. I just didn't know how I was going to carry on with this. I was not in a positive place. I started stopping every time I saw the crew in a layby, just so I could talk to them. They realized this, and they stopped stopping, they stopped just being there, so I'd keep going. Then I began to get really lonely. My internal monologue started telling me this wasn't going to happen. I started to have really concrete, negative thoughts – if I stopped now, we could get the crew back to Perth and find hotels. It would be more convenient for getting home than if I pressed on into the Highlands. The fire was going out and there was nothing I could do.'

Around this point of the ride there is a piece of video footage of Broadwith creeping along, shot through heavy rain and windscreen wipers from the following van. In it, Tim Bayley, Broadwith's crew chief, can be overheard muttering through some quick maths and finishing by saying simply, 'I think we've got a problem.' Team sponsor Pete Ruffhead says, half to himself, half to the camera, 'Well done, Mike. You've given it your best shot, we're proud of you.' A quiet sat-nav voice says, 'You are doing... 11... miles an hour.'

Broadwith pulled over in a layby with the team, and said he felt it was time to stop. Bayley agreed that, if it was him, he'd stop too – and Bayley is a champion ultra rider in his own right. Given the state Broadwith was in it was hard to see him riding another 200 miles at all, never mind doing it quickly. The only person who disagreed was Broadwith's wife, Helen. 'Can you not do another 20 minutes?' she asked. Broadwith says that the question just made him indignant – he felt she didn't understand what was happening. Of course he could do another 20 minutes – that wasn't the problem, the problem was the remaining 11 hours' riding. He decided to do the 20 minutes out of something that sounds not a million miles away from spite.

And over the next 20 minutes… it stopped raining. The sun came out. He warmed up. He got to the top of a long drag and the road dropped a little. The speed picked up. And, 'I'm still there. I'm still riding. I'm still up on schedule. I can cope with this. This is something I can still do.' He went on to break the record, even though he ended up having to physically use one hand to hold his head up so he could see the road. His time was 43 hours, 25 minutes and 13 seconds – he clipped just under 40 minutes off the previous mark of Gethin Butler.

The thing that interests me most about this turning point is that if Broadwith had stopped in the layby, climbed into the back of the van while the team packed up his bike, and been driven back to Perth to become yet another failed End-to-End attempt, what would have stopped him would have been 'physical'. The point where you can't see where you're going because your neck has stopped working, when you're cold, exhausted and you've given everything you have to give. That's the end of your body's resources, and there is no coming back from that.

Except that it wasn't. This is the problem with psychology and ultra racing. When I wrote the book *Faster* I devoted a chapter to elite sports psychology and it was more or less a discrete thing – it was essential, it was complicated, but it was still clearly one of several components that you could put together in a number of configurations. An ideal athlete would get it right, but you could be successful while getting it wrong as long as everything else was good enough to pull you through. In *Faster* I mentioned a successful pro I knew who had won everything up to an Olympic medal while still being, from a sports psychology point of view, a shambles. In ultra racing it would be hard to compensate for a lack of mindset.

As Broadwith's story shows, you can't even do the basic thing of separating physical and mental. You just can't tell which is which.

The End-to-End is a good place to find that out. It's a very difficult length – around two days. A three- or four-day event will demand a plan for sleeping. In a 24–36-hour event you probably don't sleep by design at all, at least not if you're going to do well. But two days sits very darkly between them. Add to that the fact that it's firstly a record, and secondly a very good record, and the difficulties multiply. With a record, the psychology is more pressured, because you are either breaking the record or you are not. In a race you have a number of refuges in case of mediocrity – you can decide to settle for second or third, or tenth, and promise yourself you'll do better next time. You can just accept that finishing will be your victory. You can keep going and hope that those in front will falter. In a record you can't do that, so you've no choice about how hard you'll have to ride. The challenge isn't to go as fast as possible, it's to ride to schedule for as long as you can manage. This subtle twist will help you dig yourself a really deep hole. It's like riding with someone else, potentially someone faster. Probably every cyclist has had the experience of trying to hold on to the back wheel of a faster rider, never thinking much further than clinging on for the next few hundred yards. Breaking a record can be the same, except it can last for days. Broadwith wasn't even behind the pace of his 'competitor' when his crisis arrived, but he still could only look at things in the black and white manner of whether he was going to be able to hold the wheel.

It's a good record, too. It's the oldest of the UK's place-to-place records, it's the longest and as such it's become the hardest and the most sought-after. It was first ridden as a record in 1880 by C.A. Hartman and H. Blackwell, Victorian adventurers in stockings and boots on penny farthings. They battled the weather – a penny farthing rider could be reduced to walking by even a moderate headwind, and often they were. It was the same with hills, where sometimes they pushed their bikes for miles on end. And it was the same with rough road surfaces. Locals threw stones at them because bicycles in that era were such a strange sight, and of course things broke and had to be fixed by blacksmiths. It took them 12 days.

Ever since, the record has attracted the best riders, and it has sifted most of them out. Bridges have helped make the route a little shorter and faster. The roads have improved, although at the cost of making some of the busier ones quite frightening places to ride, especially through Cornwall and Devon. But all the time the riders have got faster as well, and the task of breaking the record has become harder. When Andy Wilkinson broke the record in 1990, he did so by 58 seconds.

It's not the only record. While most ultra races are races, in the UK (and a few other areas) there are records as well. There are other place-to-place records like Land's End to John O'Groats, such as London to Edinburgh, London to Liverpool, Land's End to London, London to Brighton and back. There is a record for 1,000 miles, and for a number of circuits of places like the Yorkshire Dales or the Cairngorms, some of which would count, I think, as ultra events and some of which are perhaps a bit short.

(The 1,000-mile record is invariably held by an End-to-End rider who adds the extra 160 miles after reaching John O'Groats. In 1965, Dick Poole broke the End-to-End, and set out for the extra distance. This can be completed using whatever additional roads you like, and you would usually pick them based on the conditions at the time. It means there is no set finish line. Poole completed his additional miles in 8 hours 20 minutes. Or thought he'd completed. Owing to a miscalculation by the timekeepers, he actually stopped at 998.5 miles, and so was denied a record he'd have claimed easily. Something to think about the next time you feel you've had a wasted day. The current men's 1,000-mile record holder, in two days and eight hours, is Gethin Butler, who said he'd gone on to do the extra distance because 'There's not a lot else to do up there.')

In the UK there are also records for 12 and 24 hours, although things start to get a bit complicated because there are two different governing bodies for them, and their rules are very different. Cycling Time Trials (CTT) requires that rides be done as part of an official race, and has regulations about how far apart the starting point and finishing point can be – i.e., not very. The National 24-hour Championship is a CTT event.

The older Road Records Association (RRA), which is the outfit that looks after the place-to-place records and the 1,000 miles and also has marks for 12 and 24 hours, wants records set as stand-alone events, but doesn't mind whether you do them in circuits or in a straight line. The advantage of a straight line option is, of course, that you can do it downwind. You can also set more than one record in one ride – like the End-to-End and the 1,000 miles. The big disadvantage is that the RRA loves regulations at least as much as it loves cycling – it once had a reg that banned riding on a Sunday – and organizing an RRA record attempt is not an occupation for the administratively faint of heart. I write as someone with three law degrees and who once successfully cancelled an elderly relative's Sky TV contract after he went into a nursing home, and I would still think twice before tangling with the RRA.

*

It can be difficult to disentangle the mental from the physical in the heat of a record attempt. It can also be difficult at a deeper level. If you try to tease apart the role of the central nervous system from the biochemistry and biomechanics of the blood, the heart and the muscles, it quickly becomes clear that your brain, or at any rate your central nervous system, has a role in what was long seen as the physical side of sport. Your brain's first interest in life is keeping you alive, and as such it will seemingly protect you from yourself.

Look at it this way, it's possible to die from exhaustion, but almost no one ever does. The second-placed finisher at an ultra race does not normally ride themselves into a coma chasing the winner, however much they think they want to win. I've seen plenty of riders over a huge variety of distances give what they felt was, and what looked to me like, 'everything', who were fine a few minutes or an hour after finishing.

Whether this is 'psychology' is a reasonable question. I first came across this idea in the context of South African physiologist and ultra runner Tim Noakes's central-governor theory in the 2000s. His suggestion was that when the oxygenation of your heart, and perhaps other organs, begins to fall towards dangerous levels, the motor cortex of your brain stops you from recruiting further muscle. It does this by creating the experience of fatigue, reducing the amount of muscle you can recruit so that your oxygen consumption drops. It means that – most clearly in shorter, more intense exercise than we're mainly concerned with in long distance races – while it's the availability of oxygen that limits you, it's not just the biochemistry. Your brain and central nervous system turn down the lamp to protect your body.

The clearest expression of the central governor is in shorter distances. Noakes also referred to a study of longer distance riding – though still only in the four-hour region. In that set of experiments, the exercise intensity dropped beyond the four-hour mark, despite the fact that the riders had sufficient fuel, were hydrated, and were riding at a metabolically sustainable pace. Again, the suggestion is that fatigue comes from the brain, not from the muscles. In this instance the feeling of fatigue is the central governor implementing a pacing strategy designed to protect. The brain wants to maintain body homeostasis, or equilibrium, so that energy availability continues in prolonged exercise, and it starts to protect that even before the availability of glycogen (the form of carbohydrate stored in the muscles) begins to run short. As with shorter, more intense exercise, the motor cortex reduces the amount of muscle utilized.

You can see this 'anticipatory regulation' if you set a group of subjects the task of riding a time trial in an environmental chamber at a high temperature – they don't set off at a normal pace and get slower as the event progresses and their body temperature increases; rather, they're slower from the beginning. And not because of a conscious decision – they just can't recruit the same volume of muscle fibres.

Noakes also pointed to the Comrades Marathon (a South African 56-mile running event), where runners regularly manage to increase their pace towards the end as they try to beat the 12-hour finishing time limit. If the exhaustion came from the muscles, and they were running as fast as they physically could, this just wouldn't be possible.

The reality might be that the brain, aware that the actual danger is over and that the finish is near, allows the pace to increase.

In his book *Endure*, Alex Hutchinson explores a lot of this, often at a more applied level. Perhaps the most captivating example he offered in this area was of Diane Van Deren. Van Deren is a very successful ultra runner, specializing in very long races. She was the first woman to complete the 430-mile Yukon Arctic Ultra, and broke the record for the Mountains-to-Sea trail in North Carolina in 2012, an event that took three weeks.

What made her unusual (or perhaps even more unusual) was that owing to an operation to remove a small section of her brain that was causing her to have severe epileptic seizures, she has no ability to judge the passing of time. She has no awareness of day 10 of a race being any different from day 1, day 5 or day 15. She has no ability to process how long she's been running, or how long she has still to go. She just runs in the moment. She credits this ability/disability with having made her a much better runner (pre-surgery she ran long distances because she found it prevented her seizures, but not to the sort of level she did afterwards), specifically because pacing is no longer something she really does, or can even attempt.

What is less clear, to me at any rate, is the interaction between conscious and unconscious regulation. It seems likely that an inability to process time that stems from literally having a bit of your brain missing ought to affect the central governor. But I also notice that despite the very demanding nature of Van Deren's races, she hasn't yet run herself to death, which might suggest that either there is still an element of anticipatory regulation, or that the central governor is not the only protection. Bear in mind that her feet were so painful towards the end of the Mountains-to-Sea event that she started out each day crawling until the endorphins kicked in enough to let her stand up – it's not as if she lacked commitment.

(An additional effect of the operation was to remove the sense of spatial awareness that would let her read a map. On unsupported ultras, if she comes to a fork in the path she leaves a pink ribbon at the turn, tries one direction until it's clear that it's right or wrong, and if it's wrong, runs back till she finds the ribbon, then goes the other way. A *Runner's World* profile christened her 'The disoriented express', which is a joke I like but which I really hope she doesn't mind. But I don't suppose she'll be tracking them down.)

At an even simpler level, in *Endure* Hutchinson also points to some of the East African endurance runners (again, we're looking at sub-ultra-type race durations like the standard marathon). Often they race with confidence that feels foreign to athletes like me – instead of nice conservative pacing, there's an increased tendency towards self-belief and the conviction that today might just be the day when you'll be the athlete you've always wanted to be. Instead of primly watching the 'faster' athletes head off up the road, they go with them on the basis that perhaps this time it will work. And not infrequently it does.

That reminded me of the way 24-hour pacing used to work. The traditional approach was just the same as my first 12-hour – set off fast and hope to hang on. I can look back at it and scoff, but some of the pre-power-meter riders who approached the races that way for decades covered an awful lot of distance. And perhaps in the two 12-hours I raced that way I was just unlucky. If it had been 'my day', I'd have blasted through the benchmark 300 miles barrier and still finished feeling like a god, rather than feeling like I was about to be a statistic.

There are other perspectives on this area. The connection between mental and physical goes both ways. Your body will affect your mind, and your mind can do the reverse. You can see this very straightforwardly if you look at what happens to an athlete trying to perform when they're under an external stress – in fact, I wrote a whole book about it, *The Hour*, which was about my ultimately unsuccessful attempt to break the world hour record.

It certainly wasn't set up as an experiment, and I'd count very little about the whole experience as a success, but it was impossible not to notice my physical ability declining as the stress of organizing the event, funding it and testing equipment for it grew. It's a project that would normally involve a team of 10–20 people and a substantial budget, and when I tried to do it with the help of my girlfriend and a coach at Manchester Velodrome, I discovered what all those people I didn't have would have been doing – they would have been taking stress off me, the rider, so I could actually train, recover, repeat and race without ending up on my bike at 11 p.m. because it was the only hour in the day that was left.

One of the phrases I overuse as a coach today is, 'There's no such thing as a non-physical stress.' That's actually a little off to one side of what I mean, which is that there's no such thing as a stress that won't have an effect on the key physical outcomes, but that version is not as neat, or quite as irritating when your coach repeats it every 20 minutes. Stress is something that builds over time, it has hormonal consequences. Shorter-term mental fatigue, as a thing in and of itself, also has at least some role. If you set someone a mental challenge before setting them off to ride a bike – let's say you make them play Tetris for an hour – they don't ride as fast.

That comes with an interesting possible caveat, which is that in an experiment by sports scientist Samuele Marcora, he found that professional and amateur athletes responded differently. In one of his experiments subjects were presented with a screen that displayed the names of colours spelled out in letters of another colour – so 'blue' could be written in a red font – and had to press a button corresponding to the display colour not the named colour. That was followed by a 5-km all-out run. There were controls: some tests looked at a blank screen, some had colours and fonts that matched. For a start the pros were better at the mis-matched colour game, and for a finish their run times were unaffected by it. Amateurs were over 4% slower. So either pro athletes get better at dealing with the mental element, or their innate mental durability is why they're pro athletes. It also raises the question of whether mental training – like the colours game – could produce a benefit in physical outcome.

Perhaps you could make training more effective by incorporating boring, repetitive mental challenges, either before or during training. If you think riding a turbo trainer is dull, I'm totally confident that we in the coaching community can devise ways to make it worse. What might save you is that most of the more convincing work in the area is on either non-training or quite non-specifically trained subjects. I think there's a good chance that normal training is boring enough to press all the buttons-of-boring that you might usefully press.

As a result of his research, Marcora's take is a little different from Noakes's. His work suggests that an athlete simply decides when they've had enough. The traditional way to measure effort level in sport is the Borg scale, which runs from 6 (very, very mild) to 20 (absolutely maximal). In this model, when the athlete reaches 20, they stop. If they go into the event mentally fresh, they start lower on the scale and last longer before they get to 20. If they're better motivated, the effort level feels lower from the start and it takes longer to get to 20. But in any instance, the stopping point is a conscious acceptance of 'defeat'.

You can debate how much difference there really is between central governor and conscious stopping. In both models you exercise, the exercise produces signals you interpret as fatigue, and you stop – the sensations are the same, the result is the same. The most significant difference is whether you're consciously involved in running up the white flag, and ultimately that doesn't make much difference to the outcome because the fatigue signals and how they're interpreted are key.

Issues of motivation and pacing influence both. Both can potentially translate from the shorter distance efforts that most lab experiments use to the longer distance events. While the physical demands of the longer events are different, and the sensations of fatigue are different, there still comes a point where you reach your limit and it's hard to see any reason why that threshold isn't determined in the same way.

I've always found the idea of a central governor or similar persuasive, just because, on an anecdotal and purely individual basis, I've seen day to day variations in fitness and form that would be hard to explain in purely biological terms. I've found that even the most intense race effort isn't something I struggle to recover from – in truth I've always suspected that I've got physiological headroom I've never really exploited, and the most reasonable explanation for that would be that it's not just pure physiology that determines the outcome. But it's a very difficult hypothesis to really test. It's not hard to find exercise scientists who still firmly believe that it's down to the biochemistry of what's happening in the muscles and the blood, and that the brain, conscious or otherwise, is nothing more than a bystander.

*

The more straightforwardly conscious contribution of your brain can be equally problematic. One of the things that every rider I've ever spoken to about ultra riding has said is that there's a lot of time to think, and that thinking is a very dangerous occupation for anyone trying to rack up mileage.

Despite my having had a long career in bike racing, the conscious psychology of long distance riding was quite new. In shorter events, the problems tend to come before the event. If you're riding a short distance race – anything up to a few hours – most of your dangerous thinking comes before the event. You can call it nerves (a 'negative' way to look at it) or excitement (more 'positive') or you can call it 'an optimal state of pre-race arousal' (which is what you're aiming for, and certainly what you call it when the team sports psychologist asks).

It meant that most of the psychological interventions I've previously encountered have to do with relaxation, with working through positive mental feedback loops – 'What happens if one of my rivals is faster than me?' 'You can only control yourself – you've done the training, your current fitness numbers are better than they've ever been, and you've got years of experience. Concentrate on your own race.' I can lecture for sustained periods about the need to prioritize the process of preparation and racing, rather than thinking about the result. I can do race visualization exercises and relaxation exercises, and draw diagrams of my strengths and weaknesses. (I once mapped out my shortcomings as an athlete with such persuasive accuracy that my sports psychologist stopped coming to the meetings.)

Some of this transfers up to ultra; quite a lot of it does not. That's just the length of the event – if a short event is 90% planning and 10% execution, ultras can go a long way towards the inverse. For example, visualization clearly remains useful – the idea of closing your eyes and imagining the event, or parts of the event. If you can summon the feelings, the sounds and the visuals, then you can rehearse aspects of an event before you see them for real. As a short distance rider, I'd visualize starting efforts, or particular corners or climbs. If I'd seen the key points in the race before I got there, it was easier to get it right in the heat of the moment.

I'm in so deep that I'd actually find it hard to imagine preparing for a significant bike race of any distance without doing it. It's quite relaxing, it helps dispel some of the nagging anxieties that float around in the back of my head waiting to pop up in full Dolby surround when I try to go to sleep, and it does this just because you can confront those thoughts head-on and try to decide how you feel about them, rather than just feeling buffeted by them.

For my first 24-hour, I thought about the night sections – I'd never raced at night before, and I'd be 12 hours in by the darkest bits. I asked Mike where the support teams would be based, and where the food hand ups would be. I tried to visualize Mike or one of my other helpers looming out of the dark holding out bottles and energy gels. I tried to see how that would look with street lights, or on a country lane. I checked the course on Google Street View, so that I felt I already half-knew the roads, and looked for signposts, distinctive houses and even trees that would mean I would know more or less where I was, because nothing is more stressful on that kind of race than not being sure where you are and when the next event – maybe a turn, or a roundabout or a village – might be.

Partly that's just traditional planning, but mainly it's mopping a few of the smaller stressors out of the race itself. But I'd enter a significant caveat – it's a lot easier to recreate in your mind something you've already seen or experienced.

Ultra riders usually have less experience of all the aspects of a race, because they didn't do one every weekend for years on end as they came up through the junior ranks. They don't live through multiple mistakes and triumphs. Ultras are less consistent. The feelings you experienced in one might be very different from the next. To effectively visualize a very long race requires considerable imagination. With my relative lack of experience, and total lack of recent experience, it was hard to effectively summon the sensations that I'd have after 20 hours of non-stop racing. I knew about the potential issues, but if six things are going wrong at once, the exact recipe matters quite a lot.

It's similar with things like scenario planning. Pre-planned responses to foreseeable events (if 'x' befalls me, I shall do 'y') look as if they should work just as well for a long race as for a short. But the number of scenarios increases exponentially as the length of the event goes up. Planning for a short distance time trial involves things like punctures, overcooking the pacing early on, what to do if a time check shows you're leading, or what to do if the race is very tight. It very much doesn't involve figuring out how to charge your bike lights when you cross the border into Switzerland and discover that, contrary to everything you've been told, the power sockets are different. You think you've planned for everything? No, you haven't.

I may as well admit now that while my plan had been to do a 24-hour out of curiosity, I ended up doing two. The first out of curiosity, the second, a year later in 2024, at least partly because I felt like I'd learned a lot from the first one and didn't want to waste it. And, having decided to do that, I realized that the second one was a further learning opportunity in itself – there were different options available for things like nutritional and pacing strategies that I'd wondered about first time round, and a second race would be a chance to experiment a bit further. Having done one race, I wanted to build on it, and having done two I'd be better equipped for a third, and so on into the ultra mire.

Even if you're an experienced racer, your experience can be surprisingly narrow. Christoph Strasser had won six editions of the Race Across America (RAAM) before he entered the Transcontinental Race (TCR) as his first major unsupported event. As we'll see, the difference between supported and unsupported racing is profound – it runs through all lengths and styles of event. Do you have a team to help you? Or are you completely on your own with nothing but a bike and a distant destination?

Strasser has won RAAM six times – a supported race with a full crew of maybe eight people. A regular RAAM rider told me, a few years ago, that if Strasser was on the start line, the whole thing was a week-long race for second – and Strasser is genuinely that good. But despite being the world's best supported ultra racer at the point where his TCR entry went in, he told me simply, 'I was very afraid before my first TCR. My biggest strength is that I'm a team player. I like to hand control to the crew, then I can just push the pedals and stay awake. The crew decide eating, drinking, they write down the calories in and the fluid in, they work out what I've had and what I need. So I was afraid to be out there alone. There were going to be so many things I suddenly had to do for myself. Had I drunk enough? Do I need to eat? Where is the next gas station going to be, where does the route go next, do I need to charge my phone...? I would be thinking all the time.'

To find a perspective outside my own head, I talked to Josephine Perry, a chartered sports psychologist, about the issues around long events. I spoke to her via Zoom, and found myself thinking that I'd quite like her permanently in a corner of my laptop screen just for the air of calm rationality she gives off.

'Normally,' she said, 'people never get stopped by the things that they expect. The biggest problems are usually things that they've never imagined.' She agreed that planning matters. 'You have a threat system. We all react to things – imagine being followed down a deserted street on a quiet night. The feeling of threat kicks in very fast – but actually we need to respond, and that's much slower, because that comes from the logical part of the brain, not the emotional part. The emotional reaction might be to throw your bike off a mountain, the logical one is to sit down, have a gel and work out what to do. Some people deal with that by things like an ideal "mentor" – "What would Madonna do?" might not be quite right for you, but there's probably someone.

'The other thing you can do is plan – go through every scenario you can think of, because if you've planned for it, your threat system is less likely to kick in.' Even if you can't cover everything, you can at least thin the sources of potential panic down a little.

The preparation phase can have other psychological ramifications. The logistics for a long event can be daunting, especially if it's a supported record attempt. Ultra records are not often the work of large pro teams – almost invariably the logistics will be dealt with by the athlete, maybe with a couple of friends or a partner. If it's a supported event, you have to find a support team – maybe as many as 10 people – book flights, book hotels, vehicle rental, visas, source equipment, buy food, and a lot of other things besides. And you have to pay for it. The chances are that you need to find the money by getting some sponsors, and you'd be surprised how few people or organizations are willing to give you many thousands of pounds on the basis of a promise to have a go at riding from A to distant B faster than anyone else. So that needs a pitch, publicity and social media commitments. If you do find some help, then there's a relationship to be managed, personal appearances and interviews to fit in and branding to incorporate.

When Leigh Timmis set about breaking the European West-to-East record, from Lisbon to the Ural mountains, he was in exactly the position of being his own management. A two-week-long ride that crossed the Russian border was especially challenging, from obvious things like crew and visas, to the less expected problem that he had to organize an entirely separate support vehicle for the Russian elements of the ride because they couldn't take an RV across the border. They had to swap everything over at the frontier, and have the Western leg RV repatriated while the record attempt continued. He said that trying to juggle all of that alongside the need to fit in quite a high training volume and doing some long UK-based rides with his team to rehearse the support and logistics, was a significant psychological challenge in itself, even before he set off across Europe.

He managed to use the stresses of all that as part of his psychological preparation for the event – and there were numerous times when he says he snapped. During one lab test, where he was given a four-hour ride of gradually ramping intensity, on a stationary bike in a plain, featureless lab with no company or entertainment, he got so angry that he punched the handlebars hard enough to spray his own blood over the empty white wall in front of him. The test in question was not, as he'd been told, physiological – it was a mental-resilience test in the form of an ambush, done just to see how he'd react to a physically draining, psychologically difficult situation, and, more importantly, show him how he'd react to it.

He had similar experiences on the rehearsal rides. There were instances when the support team got stuck in traffic, times when they'd had to leave him riding on his own because the route was too narrow for the vehicle. Again, how you respond to things like that gives a sports psychologist the sort of insight that they won't get by giving you a questionnaire. The challenge for the psychologist is to find the strategies that you can use to get yourself under control again – probably not 'What would Madonna do?', but that sort of thing.

I did take one thing much more directly from Leigh. I interviewed him on stage at a book launch event, and afterwards helped him carry some of his kit to his car, including wheeling his bike. I noticed that on the bars there was a small sticker that read, 'The best you can be right now'. I liked the sentiment – while perfection is a nice idea, there are also times when you shouldn't demand things of yourself that you can't do. There are times when your best feels like it's less than you wanted, but it is still all you should aim for. If you do that, then maybe things will get better, maybe they'll get worse, but it's not something you'll gain very much by worrying about. At least, while you wait for things to resolve themselves one way or another, you're still moving.

Despite a lifelong dislike of inspiring mottos, I made an identical sticker for my own bike. And there have been times in the long races when it helped – it felt a lot less trite in the hour or two after dawn when I was feeling at a low ebb. If nothing else, having the statement written down meant it had a certain default status – if that wasn't how I was going to think about things, it was at least my starting point. If I didn't like it, I'd have to decide why it was wrong. And it made it all right to back off a bit if that was what I needed to do to get through the next 20 minutes.

However good your preparation, the hard bits of a long ride are still hard. They're unpredictable, they potentially last a long time. In my first 24-hour Championships, my computer packed up at around 2 a.m. – I'd rigged up an extra battery for it, but more than 13 hours of torrential rain had forced moisture into the connections and it eventually gave up. For the first couple of hours after that I had a rough idea of the time, because I knew how long the lap I was riding took. But then I lost count of even that because I failed to successfully count to three. (That's ultra riding for you.)

After that... well, the next landmark was dawn. It got light very slowly, very greyly, and I was only really aware of it when I realized that I could see a kerb that had been impossible to see all night, and which had made me very nervous every time I rode that stretch of road. 'What time is dawn?' I wondered. 'Four? Five?' I had, what, nine or ten hours to go?

'What time is it?' I shouted at Mike at a hand up. 'Don't worry about it,' he said. That sort of thing puts you in a box, because you can't shout back, 'But I am worrying about it,' without blowing your cover as a psychological inadequate.

But not long after that, passing through a village, I saw a man in his driveway washing a car. 'Aha,' I thought. 'No one washes a car on a Sunday morning before, what, 8 a.m.? Maybe 7.30?' That left me about six hours to go. Which I was all right with, at least until I remembered that six hours was my longest pre-race training ride, and six hours hadn't seemed all that brief then. But I was sufficiently on top of myself that I could calmly look forward to an imminent morning stop. It would be just a few minutes for a new skinsuit, a change to put on some dry shoes and socks, but it would make me feel better, I'd get a better idea of how I was doing in the race, because while the last I'd heard I was in second place, that update had been hours earlier, in full darkness. Then it would be time to settle into being the best I could be (for now) for the last five and a bit hours and with a bit of luck a ride towards a not-too-traumatic top three or four placing.

It was about an hour's worth of the lap after that that the team passed my recharged computer back to me. The time was 5 a.m. It was utterly crushing. It produced a perfect emotional threat-response that Josephine Perry could have put in her scrapbook, which I felt flush hotly through my whole body before any sort of rational analysis even started to think about happening. The first urge I had was to go and find the freak show who'd been washing his car at, what, four in the morning? Where was there to go in Shropshire at four o'clock on a wet Sunday morning that demanded a freshly washed car? The second was to quit, because suddenly I'd got nine hours to go. And nine is essentially half of 24. In terms of the general duress of the thing it's probably rather more.

I'd been expecting five in the morning to be difficult – the closest thing I'd done recently to a 24-hour bike race was a week-long offshore sailing race. Reliably, the hardest part of every day on an offshore race is just after dawn. You'd made it through the hours of darkness, and the adrenaline that propped you up started to subside. It would be light, but it would still be cold, it would still be grey, and the dawn you'd waited for would have happened so slowly that you barely noticed.

But what I couldn't have planned for in the bike race was the sudden kick in the teeth from a time point of view. You can put up with a lot as long as it happens gradually. In the early 12-hour events I did, I got to hell inch by inch – if anything had happened suddenly, I'd have been in much more danger of getting off and giving up. My 24-hour races have never been as miserable as either of those, but getting my Garmin back was an actual shock. The best I could be at that point wasn't amazing, but it kept me going long enough to regroup.

In any long event there will be difficult bits, though. What matters more is how you deal with them. There is an extent to which ultra riding is the art of keeping going. When I asked one multi-week rider what it was about him that made him so well suited to ultra racing, I was expecting an answer that had something to do with his physical ability, but what he said was, 'An ability to believe that things are going to get better.' In fact, one definition of what constituted a properly long event that I came up with was, 'A ride long enough that it can get worse, and then get better again.'

(This would probably make a 12-hour too short to be a long ride, since there's not much time to get out of a hole unless you start digging it very fast as soon as you start. But I still think a 12-hour is a long ride, so it's not a perfect definition.)

Multi-day races are a little different in scale. Fiona Kolbinger won the TCR in 2019, becoming the first woman to win the event overall. She told me, 'From day three onwards it's about suffering. There are no watts coming out of your legs, it's not about being strong or about being fast, it's about keeping going. About keeping going and not being slow. I'm lucky, I can not-be-slow for a really long time.'

You have to look at your motivations – why are you doing this in the first place? What's your purpose? The more powerful that is, the more it connects to other people, the stronger it is and the better you can use it to pull through the hard bits. The will to win or break a record can be very effective, for the right person. The right person is someone with the physical ability to actually go fast enough, and the competitive urge that makes winning enough in and of itself. Christoph Strasser, for example, talks about winning, competing, tracking his competitors and was 100% committed to the idea that what he was doing was racing. I find this easy to understand.

For others, the motivation is something else. In fact, even if you're a contender, if you've had a bad event and you've accepted you're not going to win, there at least has to be some other motivation to continue.

At some point in a long race – let's say that point is four days into RAAM, you've got saddle sores, your neck has collapsed and you're riding in a neck brace, you've started having hallucinations, and you're really, really hating life – your brain is going to perk up and say, 'Why are you doing this? This is a stupid thing to do, and no one is making you do it. You could stop.' And you have to have an answer. There's next to no money involved, there's not a lot of glory – it's a small amateur world that only occasionally attracts wider attention. Your family will almost certainly rather you didn't do it. Your employer will do their best to ignore it, because otherwise it will give them all sorts of panic attacks about having a recruitment procedure that let you through the net undetected. So, really, why?

Ultra athletes fold their motivations in so early during the process that they are almost in danger of forgetting them, despite their importance. They become unspoken. For some, it's 'just' about proving they can do something – the George Mallory 'Because it's there' justification for attempting to climb Everest. You want to do it just because you can, as a test of your own character. It's like a 3,000-km version of throwing a ball of paper across the office into the bin. The misery, perceived and actual, would be a major attraction because you'd be able to tell yourself you'd withstood something exceptional, you'd endured. Whatever you did from then on in life, you'd be able to say you'd survived. However rough things were in life afterwards, at least you wouldn't be trying to find a part for your hydraulic brakes at six o'clock on a Sunday morning in Montenegro. It would give you something to be proud of. It might even improve your image of yourself.

Or – and I think this is slightly different – you might want to set yourself a challenge that you think you'll be good at. There the idea wouldn't be to suffer. It would be to triumph, in some respect. You might even feel a duty to do it – I did my first 12-hour because I was very good at shorter distances, so I felt I'd got no choice but to see what would happen if I moved up in duration. It was a racing scene and a career I was committed to, and I wanted to see it through. I didn't feel I'd got a duty to my talent to push myself to the limits, but I can understand why someone might feel that way. If you're a good athlete, you're always aware of others who work just as hard, but who weren't as lucky with their opportunities or their genes. There's a feeling you shouldn't squander your good fortune. This can shade into a more negative mindset – a feeling of external pressure that you've invented for yourself. (One of the most useful things anyone ever said to me in my career was simply, 'Michael, no one cares.')

Your cause might be as 'negative' as proving someone wrong. Before my first 24-hour, there was no shortage of social media experts declaring I wouldn't make it past the first 100 miles. I've got used to this sort of thing over the years, and I'd committed to the race weeks before it became public knowledge so by that point I didn't really pay much attention. But I know riders for whom it would be rocket-fuel. The criticism doesn't have to be well founded. No less distinguished a rider than Fiona Kolbinger told me that a lot of her motivation comes from showing people that she knows what she's doing, in cycling and in life – 'It's the same with a scientific paper. If my methodology is better, I want people to know that. Same with surgery, same with cycling. People think, "Oh, she's just a woman, she'll go off and get pregnant at some point and then just disappear."'

I asked psychologist Josephine Perry what she thought of that sort of attitude, and she said simply, 'If it works for you, use it. I'm not sure there's really any such thing as a negative motivation.'

One of the other things I've noticed as I talked to riders and read about ultra challenges is that there are a lot of competitors who are recovering from some trauma – bereavement, addiction, depression. I'm fortunate enough not to have been through any of those, but I can see why ultra racing might click. It's something you can lose yourself in, it can be a meditation, a less harmful addiction, a confirmation of self-esteem. It's a positive thing to survive. That can also tie into something more external – raising money for a charity, say. You can't stop because you've bought into something that's bigger than you. Or raising awareness of a cause – which might feel a bit nebulous, but if you're sufficiently invested in it, it will work the same way. If it's a supported event and a lot of people have given up time to help you, you might simply not want to let your team down. On an unsupported race you might not be able to face the thought of your dot stopping moving, and the feeling that you've lost a connection to a host of anonymous but well-meaning strangers on the internet, strangers who are sincerely wishing you the best.

It can be weirdly specific – I'd have packed up and gone home in my second (incredibly horrible) 12-hour were it not for the knowledge that a friend of mine had been deputed to cover the race for a magazine, and he'd had to miss his daughter's eighteenth birthday party to do it. For six wretched hours I ground on because I knew I was the big story in the race from the point of view of the magazine he was writing for, and I wasn't prepared to pack up and leave him with a less newsworthy event. It just felt like a rough thing to do to a friend. At one point I vomited on my handlebars and groaned with loneliness and despair, and then immediately thought, 'David will enjoy hearing about that.'

It can also be altruistic. A theme that emerged from several of the interviews I did was just how generous ultra riders were with their knowledge, with what their experience had gained them. Ultra riding, for now at least, has a feeling of community. There's an interest in pushing the sport on together, in finding out what we're all capable of. TCR (in common with many other events) has a party for finishers – several riders talked about the need to get there for the party, to tell stories, share experiences, to be part of something, to belong.

Whatever it is, it helps if you identify it. For my first 24-hour, my main priority wasn't to win or to medal, it was to finish. My publicly stated aim before the event was, 'To still be going fast enough at the end of the 24 hours that I'm able to keep my balance.' That was all. The reason I wanted to do it was largely because I wanted to see if I could, and what would happen. But that's not actually a great justification for finishing – the post-event tale of 'what happened' could just as easily be, 'I quit at 15 hours because I'd seen a weirdo washing his car.' It doesn't keep you on your bike.

There were other things. Riding the 24-hour meant I'd finish a set of events – the 24 meant I'd done all the set time and distance events run by the UK time trialling governing body, from 10 miles to 24 hours. I've won all the other ones at some point, and I'd be lying if there wasn't a small, unexpressed hope that I'd somehow manage to at least get a medal at the 24-hour.

I also wanted to do it to become one of the people who's done a long race, because of that sense of community. I'd done a podcast about ultra riding, and found the people I interviewed for it completely inspiring. I very straightforwardly wanted to be one of them, and the entrance exam was a long ride.

And finally, by the time the event came around, and again off the back of the podcast, I'd decided to write a book about ultra riding. I didn't want to write a book that was specifically about the 24-hour, and doubly didn't want to end up writing a book about 'my personal challenge' because there are too many of them already, but it was pretty obvious that going for a long ride would be a helpful perspective. I'd have more understanding of the events, and maybe a few anecdotes. (Have I mentioned the guy washing his car?) Into the last hours of the 24, the thing I kept referring to was that I wanted to finish this because I wanted to understand it, and I didn't want to write about having tried something and failed. I think I even wanted to acquire the small bit of authority on the subject that would come from finishing.

I admitted this slightly cheap-feeling motivation to Josephine Perry, who made her 'no bad sources of motivation' comment again, but more helpfully suggested that if telling the story was a motivation, I ought to look at why I wanted to tell the story. 'Maybe you're moving the sum of knowledge on this on a little,' she suggested. 'Maybe it's a little like a PhD – you can add just a little to what we know. And perhaps you help someone else start doing it.'

The other, stupider, thing that helped was a firm belief in the sunk cost fallacy. You do get to a point where you've been riding for 20 hours and you feel like those would have been 20 hours very badly spent if you don't go on to finish the job.

Something I noticed about the final hour or two of my first 24-hour was that it never started to get easier. The last 15 minutes were less pleasant than the 15 minutes before, and those were less pleasant than the 15 before them. Something I'd suggest you never, ever say to anyone in a long event is 'You're nearly there.' It is a thought that is no use at all to someone who is trying to be the best they can be right now, and work from short-term goal to short-term goal. At that point the thing you're devoting most of your time to trying to ignore is the time left to run. If my complete set of aims and ambitions in life is just to ride consistently till I reach the next turn in five minutes' time, to keep in a neat aero position till I get there, to keep my head still, and to eat a disgusting gel somewhere between here and there without being sick, a well-meaning but perspective-broadening shout of 'Almost there!' is the sort of thing that produces casualties.

It's a problem that scales up. More than one TCR rider told me that among the most difficult sections of that race, lasting well over a week, was the final 12–16 hours, just because they suddenly realized how close to the end they were. After days and days of a focus that never went much further than the next gas station, or did they need to eat, did they need to sleep, when was the next turning, is that knee niggle a problem or will it go away, they suddenly realized it was 'almost over'. All the little micro-targets that had been getting them through the days a few minutes at a time fell away and they were faced with what was still by any normal measure a huge slab of riding to get through. An ending that was almost irrelevant to everyday coping becomes almost overwhelming.

In her book *Where There's a Will*, Emily Chappell wrote about the final hours of her winning TCR ride in 2016, down a roasting-hot road along the coast to the Dardanelles strait. It feels like a collapse in slow motion, or a fading away, as the accumulated pains and the exhaustion start to become a very gradual ending. 'I'd guess at what the current total [distance to go] might be as pessimistically as I could, hoping to surprise myself when it turned out to be less, but my estimates turned out to be disappointingly accurate.' She ended up stopping to sleep behind a crash barrier with 'just' 50 miles to go because she had no choice. It was the adrenaline-depleted opposite of a sprint finish.

Professor Greg Whyte is a sports scientist who has, among other things, helped a very large number of celebrity endurance challenges – if you've ever seen someone spending days doing something for the BBC's Children in Need charity, chances are that Whyte was one of the coaching and support team. He's also an athlete, having ridden a team relay Race Across America. He's seen an awful lot of people, both athletes and non-athletes, through some long efforts. He's the sort of man who's very clear about the things he's learned over the years. 'The end is the hardest,' he told me, simply. 'Especially in 24-hour challenges. That last hour is so difficult. You look at the clock, and you just can't believe how little it's moved since you last looked. I tell the support team that I don't ever want to hear the phrase "Nearly there", simply because they're not nearly there. It might be the last hour, but that's a long time.'

There can be other patterns. Chappell told me that she often had a crisis of some sort around eight days in, and for her that's a danger point as far as giving up is concerned. 'By eight days,' she said, 'as well as the fatigue there'll always be some legitimate reason, like a medical reason, to drop out.' Other riders said similar things, but the danger zones seem to be personal. It's not uncommon for riders who're doing the events with a competitive mindset to start too hard and keep pushing for the first couple of days to try to establish a lead, only to have a horror show around day three.

The idea of an excuse to stop – Chappell's medical reason – matters more than you might think. On a long ride, there are countless reasons to stop. One of Mike Broadwith's justifications for stopping when he didn't on the End-to-End was that it would be easier for the crew to get home if he stopped not far from Perth. TCR riders have to ride past railway stations every day, any one of which would be a quick, easy route home. When you're sleep deprived and lonely, resisting excellent justifications to stop while your brain shouts, 'But it's the only sensible thing to do!' is hard.

There are smaller cycles as well. Chappell struggles with afternoons. 'I don't know why. But they just feel like the end of the world – I'm slow and pathetic and I hate myself and everything on my bike. But it's a pattern. I always feel like that. It's become part of my race strategy – from the moment I get up, say 3 a.m., till lunch time I'm flying. After that, for a while, I go really slowly, hoping no one sees me hobbling along on the little chainring. Then when it gets dark, I seem to get a second wind of some sort. It's like the opposite of being solar powered.'

Research on the mood swings of RAAM riders found repeatable patterns there too. A relay team of four (one of whom was Greg Whyte, which is a committed bit of research) were asked to complete questionnaires during their race. They ranked emotions including anger, calmness, confusion, depression, happiness, fatigue, tension and vigour, and the riders classified each of those according to the emotions they experienced when riding well (functional) or badly (dysfunctional). It's worth noting that one of the riders associated 'anger' and 'tension' with riding well, which isn't typical.

The pattern was interesting. Day one was the best. Fuelled by enthusiasm, by carbohydrate, by a good night's sleep and by not being in agony from a saddle sore the size of an egg, the reported emotional state was as perfect as something that subjective can ever be. The worst day of the seven days the race took was day two, and it was the worst by miles. On day one 100% of responses to the questionnaire showed a functional mood. By day two, in an almost total reversal of mood, 85% of responses were dysfunctional.

Things then got better. Day three was 60% functional, day four was 71%, day five was 67%. The penultimate day, day six, functional responses dropped sharply to 40% before going back up to 57% on the last day. Clearly that was one group of riders. It was a relay rather than a solo effort, and there are some other considerations for relays – there are more personal interactions, and the performance is neither your total responsibility nor your sole achievement. Above all, it's less physically demanding. You can sleep a lot more, you can eat a lot more relative to your energy expenditure.

*

But the emotional profile seems to fit with quite a few solo riders I've talked to. Day one – easy. Day two – horrible, partly as a result of hitting day one too hard because you felt good. Then better. Then worse. Then, finally, better, but not as good as you'd expect for the final 'sprint to the line' – or, in most cases, stagger to the line. Knowing the patterns can help deal with the swings.

But how you cope is highly individual. How individual? One of my favourite interviews was with RAAM rider Shu Pillinger. She was one of the most articulate riders I've met, as well as someone who could be both honest and funny about her races, good and bad. As a supported rider, she was always at least to some extent relying on her team to provide some motivation. 'And they did some weird stuff,' she told me. 'Toward the end, I wanted to be talked to all the time on the radio. They were in the car going, "I want to sleep but this woman on the bike is demanding a story." They read me stuff from Facebook, then they stopped at a gas station and bought some really dodgy soft porn paperback [like there's any other kind of soft porn paperback in a gas station]. Then they started reading it out to me over the radio, except they did it in different accents and I had to try to guess the accent.'

Like I say, whatever gets you through it.

3

The Never-Exceed Speed

Having picked 24-hour racing as my new pastime, the question was what could I bring with me from the short distance world? I had a bike – a Specialized Shiv time trial bike – which was a start, and some kit like wheels, helmets, race suits. I knew what I knew from the 12-hour races, both the good and the bad. So I understood that as the race gets longer, things seem to get exponentially more complicated. But to me the biggest question was physical. What did I, as a decent athlete from a 'normal' background, have in terms of actual physiological ability when it came to this, very different-feeling, way to go racing?

My strong suspicion was that some of the things that made me good when I was a pro were going to be active handicaps. A short race is an intensely physical thing. To grossly oversimplify, a short time trial race is a question of how hard you can pedal, the power you can put through the back wheel over the length of the event. In a short race, I know the major issues of physiology that decide how fast I'll go, and I also know how I might push those limits a bit further away. These events, the ones I was used to, are about moving oxygen to the muscles. That's almost the whole ball game. There are some other details – how efficiently your muscles use that oxygen is probably the main one – but the bigger picture is just raw oxygen shifting, which is about heart and blood and circulation. I understand that, and I understand how to make my body better at it through training.

Long distance events are at a much lower intensity, so there's a lot less oxygen needed. But that left me uncertain as to what the new limits were going to be. Was it 'fuel economy', the question of how much energy you get out in muscle power for each gram of energy you put in in terms of sugar and oxygen? Was it all just going to hinge on nutrition and how much you can eat? Was it something else entirely?

If you want to understand what the physical limits are, it helps to understand at least a little about how your body produces movement in the first place. It's worth saying at the outset that this isn't a simple engineering solution. No one would have designed human exercise physiology as a rational solution to anything – it's a sometimes chaotic-feeling mix of biochemistry and physics. But even so, while the different systems go together in a way that might not be obviously elegant, they do at least work quite effectively. I suppose that's evolution for you.

The basic starting point is that fibres in a muscle contract in response to the presence of the adenosine triphosphate or ATP molecule. That's the only thing that prompts the muscle to do anything at all, and it would be an accurate if very pedantic response to the question 'What limits physical performance?' to say that in any circumstances and any event from weightlifting to cycling round the world, it's the availability of ATP. At any given time there are just a very few grams of ATP in your body, and that is only enough to generate a few seconds of activity. The challenge to keeping moving is making more of it, which happens constantly in the muscles.

There are two ways to make ATP, either with or without using oxygen, so that's aerobically or anaerobically. To do it aerobically, oxygen combines with fuel in the forms of fat and carbohydrate to produce ATP, carbon dioxide and hydrogen. The carbon dioxide is exhaled, and the hydrogen combines with oxygen to make water, which is released into the bloodstream and exits as urine, sweat or as vapour in your breath.

To make ATP anaerobically, you just use carbohydrate. It's a less efficient reaction than the aerobic equivalent – for each gram of carbohydrate consumed it produces something like one fifteenth of the ATP. Like the aerobic reaction, this produces hydrogen, but since there's no oxygen for it to combine with, this time instead of water it produces a substance called lactate as a means of disposing of it. Lactate is traditionally the source of all evil in exercise. ('The lactate will be literally setting his legs on fire!' as a friend of mine once said while commentating on a sprint event at the 2020 Olympics.) It's not evil – it's just part of the energy cycle. Lactate becomes a fuel source when oxygen is available, or it can be transported to the liver and converted to glycogen. It does a host of other clever things as well, like moving energy from an inactive muscle to an active one. You wouldn't want to be without it.

The reputation of lactate as being a problem substance is probably not based on anything much more than it having been one of the early physiological markers that scientists identified and measured, so it got the blame for everything. The high concentrations of it that you find during sprint efforts were assumed to be the cause of the muscle-burning fatigue that makes the life of the sprinter or high-intensity interval trainer so uncomfortable. That's not really the case.

It's woefully inconsistent that it also used to get the blame for delayed onset post-exercise muscle soreness, when the most obvious thing about that phenomenon is that it is at its worst following long, low-effort events like marathons where lactate concentrations remain low because the anaerobic contribution to ATP production is low. Of course, you still hear riders talking about going for a ride the day after a race 'to get the lactate out of my legs', and they are wrong about this. I've even heard people saying they're going out for a ride the day after a 24-hour to clear the lactate, and for most of a 24-hour your lactate levels are probably, if anything, lower than they would be sitting on a sofa. But it's always nice to go for a ride, and it's even nicer if you've found a justification for going very slowly and stopping for a coffee break.

While there is a very real-feeling contrast between aerobic endurance and anaerobic sprint effort levels, the practical division between aerobic and anaerobic is not particularly clear cut. There is lactate produced from anaerobic production of ATP in the muscles all the time, even at rest, which is recycled into energy.

Let's assume that at rest your lactate level might be 1.2 mmol/ml. Low and moderate levels of effort might actually push this number down a bit, maybe to around 1.1 mmol/ml, as the blood flow starts to increase. If you keep increasing the level of effort – imagine doing a gradual ramp up of intensity on a home trainer, or accelerating very gradually over 10 or 15 minutes along a flat road – the level will stay the same for a while, but eventually it will begin to increase.

This point where it starts to increase, where the line graph of lactate concentration against effort starts to kink upwards, is lactate threshold. From that point onwards lactate concentration will gradually increase as the effort level rises. That's until you get to a second point, where it stops increasing gradually and begins to increase at a rate that might not be strictly speaking exponential, but looks like it on the graph.

I'd say it feels exponential in the legs as well, had I not just explained that lactate doesn't make your legs hurt at all. It's telling how hard-wired the lactate myths are that I know this and can't quite shake off the idea. If you have to pick one thing to blame it on, potassium would be a better bet, but somehow the 'potassium burn' still doesn't sound right. What's very clear about this second upward kink in the graph is that it's the point where you switch from something you can sustain for minutes to something you can only sustain for seconds.

(The familiar cycling concept of functional threshold power or FTP is around this kink in the graph. FTP is the effort level you can sustain for an hour. It's not a physiological value as such, you don't pin it down in a lab by looking for markers in a blood test or something like that, you find it by just seeing how hard you can ride for an hour, or using a shorter all-out test (maybe 20 minutes) and making an estimate. It is, essentially, an attempt to identify this lactate turn point without taking blood samples in a lab. 'What's your FTP?' is one of those questions that a particular sort of performance-minded bike riders ask each other on a more or less continuous basis, and there's always a certain awed hush when someone reveals the FTP of a top World Tour rider.)

This second point has a variety of names – onset of blood lactate accumulation, maximum lactate steady state (because it's the last point where lactate is cleared from the blood as quickly as it's produced), or very unhelpfully, lactate threshold. This is because the actual lactate threshold isn't a very remarkable point in terms of physical sensations, and intuitively lactate threshold seems like a good name for the second, much more physically intrusive, point. Which is why alternative names for the pair are lactate threshold one (LT1) and lactate threshold two (LT2) – and that's what I call them.

In some respects it doesn't much matter what we call it, because in ultra racing it's a place you do not want to go. Ever. The only possible excuses for that level of effort are 1) being chased across Lancashire by a lion during an attempt on the Land's End to John O'Groats record, 2) feeling up for a sprint finish at the end of an ultra. They are about as likely as each other.

THE NEVER-EXCEED SPEED

But the LT1 point, the true lactate threshold at the first kink in the graph, is very relevant to ultras. If you are an ultra racer, LT1 is your never-exceed effort level. You do not go harder than this, not unless you want to pay back with interest later. There are a number of consequences to going past LT1 – the two most important are that it's the point at which you start to burn an increasing proportion of carbohydrate as fuel; the second is that it's the point where the amount of heat your body is generating starts to ramp up.

The fuel issue matters simply because you have a huge reservoir of energy stored as fat, and a tiny amount stored as carbohydrate. If you're going to use carbohydrate, you need to replace it by eating or drinking it, and there are rather tight limits on how much you can consume, especially when you're riding a bike and otherwise putting your body and digestive system through a bit of an ordeal. Heat matters for several reasons. One is that as you start to sweat it will affect your hydration levels. Another is that you get less efficient as you get warmer, and the enzymes responsible for metabolizing ATP from oxygen and fat/carbohydrate work a lot less effectively as you get warmer. So you want to stay cool as best you can.

LT1 effort level is not hard. It's well within the speed at which you can have a conversation. When I was a serious rider, my base mileage was almost entirely done just below LT1 – hours and hours of slightly dull plodding around the place, occasionally interspersed with 'proper training', i.e. efforts into the more demanding territory above. It's not a coincidence that it's such an important speed for training. It means you can train things like efficiency in the muscles or capillary density that respond to longer efforts, without creating excessive fatigue or giving you fuelling problems. For me, it's a pulse of around 140 bpm, a good 30 bpm below the 170 bpm or so I'd expect to see in a 20-minute race. In other words, if you're going long, you have to go slow, and go slow from the start. (These pulse reference points have dropped as I've grown older – when I was in my twenties, they'd have been more like 150 bpm and 185 bpm.)

These strictures can have counterintuitive effects. When Mike Broadwith set the current Land's End to John O'Groats record in 2018, he worked off a modest never-exceed effort. In a UK place-to-place record, it's not uncommon for the timekeepers to travel from the start to the finish following the rider. As Broadwith set off through the hilly early stages of the ride in Cornwall and Devon, one of the timekeepers (someone who'd seen more than their share of record attempts, good and bad) dismissed what he was seeing on the basis that any rider who was going to break the record was going to have to ride the hills in a much more attacking style. 'What's it going to be like when he gets to the Highlands?' was the question. (As we've already seen, by the Highlands he was a wreck, but he was still going, and at nearly the same speed.)

Nor is it the way people used to approach it. One of the arts of traditional, long-standing ultra events like the National 24 or Land's End to John O'Groats was the preparation of a schedule. This was often a job placed in the hands of a wise old rider. When Andy Wilkinson broke the UK 24-hour record in 1997, his schedule had been prepared by the previous record holder from 1969, Roy Cromack, who drew up schedules for 507, 515 and 525 miles. Wilkinson rode almost exactly 525 miles, despite being down on schedule early on.

Much of the art of the scheduler was working out at what rate the rider would slow down. The conventional wisdom was to start relatively fast, on the basis that since it was all going to turn to soup eventually, you'd better make sure you'd got some miles in the bank before that happened. When I did my first 12-hour, an experienced friend helped me with my schedule, which he did by a statistical meta-analysis of championship-winning 12-hour rides over the previous decade.

Of course, what he produced was a distillation of the conventional wisdom. Start faster than the target pace, and slow down at an approved rate. I no longer have a copy of the schedule, but as best as I can recall the drop-off was gradual until around eight hours, then steepened, until it recovered a bit in the final hour. I wish I still had the document, because while it wasn't much help as a schedule ('here is a huge spreadsheet of the mistakes you should make'), it was a pretty good overview of the traditional approach.

I hope I'm not being too sniffy about the traditional methods. The scheduler's art existed because in an age before power meters or even accurate computers you had to pace yourself somehow. Since the only reliable instrument you were going to have with you was a watch, the only option for that schedule was time-on-distance, and the distances were going to be to known points on the course. Things like villages, junctions and turns. Rather than a minute-by-minute update, you might have an hour between waypoints, waypoints you were going to have either to remember, or write on a bit of paper small enough to stick to your bars.

And it required judgement from the scheduler to predict how fast any given stretch of road was going to be. The schedule would try to take account of the surface, the hills, even the likely wind direction. It was performance modelling, essentially, but done by intuition rather than with GPS data and a giant spreadsheet, then implemented by a rider who was working on feel. Throw in the fact that often the earlier stages of a race were on faster main roads before the middle and latter parts of the route moved to quieter lanes, and you can see how difficult it was, and how tempting it was to 'play it safe' with an aggressive start rather than be left trying to catch up. This was years or decades away from being able to look at a screen on your bars and keep a magic number – your carefully calculated target power – within a range you'd gone to a lab to establish.

Although having gone out of my way to point all that out, it's amazing how many reports of old 12- and 24-hour time trials feature accounts of riders racing each other hard from the start, and ignoring the idea of pacing completely. In his book *The 24 Hour Story*, about the history of 24-hour racing in the UK, John Taylor praises the dominant distance rider of the 1960s, Nim Carline, not for his elegant pacing, but for his all-out aggression and his determination to intimidate other riders from the moment the timekeeper said 'go'. In an era before power meters and computers made optimizing your own race and disregarding everyone else into the simplest option, there were considerable benefits available to those who could put rivals off their game.

Nim Carline was a hard-riding Yorkshireman of a very specific mould. I doubt he'd have been much interested in an explanation of LT1. Nor, I suspect, would his equivalent today. I, on the other hand, am not that sort of rider. I was quite excited at the discovery that LT1 was a key to 24-hour pacing.

That's because for a long time I had assumed that I wouldn't really be all that well suited to ultra riding. I'd been a specialist at blasting out some biggish numbers over a shortish period. At the very top end of the graph that goes through LT1 and LT2 is something called VO2 max, which you've probably heard of, and which is a measure of your absolutely flat-out aerobic ability. Essentially it's just the maximum amount of oxygen you can breathe into your lungs, get into the bloodstream, transport to the muscles and use.

My VO2 max, when I was at my best, was among the highest measured values in the world, at over 90 millilitres of oxygen per minute per kilo of bodyweight. (An average value would have been 40–50 ml/min/kg. Most Tour de France winners are 'only' in the 80s.) My actual outside-the-lab ability was a bit of a letdown in comparison. And the reason for that was that some of the rest of my physiology wasn't all that great. I could use a great deal of oxygen flat out, but I couldn't cruise along at a high proportion of that maximum effort for very long. A world-class rider could probably ride at 85% or even 90% of their VO2 max for an hour; I never managed much more than 78%. On the graph of effort against lactate, I got to that second turn point too soon, the lactate levels went up, and that was the limit. It left me 35–40 watts down, so a little under 10%, on someone with my aerobic capacity and an equivalently good LT2.

It seemed likely, then, that the same sustainable proportion of VO2 max problem that left me marooned as a very good but not brilliant shorter distance racer would simply translate across to longer stuff. But if LT1 was the key marker, well, my LT1 was different. Historically it was very good indeed. There were points in my career when I was at my best when my LT1 was 67% of my VO2 max rather than a more commonplace 55–60%. In raw numbers, 335 watts, or at least, 335 watts a decade ago. There would have been very few riders in the world, weight-for-weight, who would have been better.

Even today my LT1 is around 290 watts, which is pretty healthy for a retired ex-bike racer. In a Zoom call with exercise physiologist Mark Burnley, I kept asking questions about how my training history, my racing experience or my age might impact my ability to ride an ultra. How might all of that affect things? 'Ultra races are physiology driven – but it's not about pushing limits. It's about staying below LT1,' he said. 'It's all reflected in LT1. That's the number that tells you how good, physiologically, you are at this. Your history, your experience, your ability – refer to LT1.'

The problem was that irrespective of all that, I could not have ridden a 24-hour at 335 watts a decade ago, nor could I do it at 290 watts today. The former would have broken the world record by about 40 miles. Even the latter would be enough to get close to the world record, and take the British record with plenty of fresh air to spare. It's a solid rule of performance modelling that if you run the model and conclude that riding straight into the record books will be easy, you've got it wrong.

(Ultra racing is not amenable to neat modelling, incidentally. The variables go up exponentially with the distance – that's the case even if you exclude all the other elements and just look at the physiology of it, the bit you'd think was most predictable. You can do all the maths you like, you'll still be wrong. You will possibly do better than pure guesswork, but that's about where you need to set your expectations as you sit down to create a spreadsheet.)

Given the target power is so low, you would imagine that riding an ultra was, physiologically speaking, pretty easy. If I take my LT1 to be around 290 watts, and knock off 15 watts for a safety margin, that would mean riding at 275 watts. This (or whatever the physiological equivalent is for you) is very easy to do. If you've been doing enough riding to stay reasonably comfortable on the bike, you can go out for three to four hours and ride along at that pace perfectly happily, with no obvious reason why you might not just keep doing this indefinitely, at least as long as you could keep fuelling it. You'd expect to get saddle sore before you'd expect to run into any physiological issues.

However. You don't flat-line your way through any race physiologically. That's true of short events – in a 20-minute event body temperature and heart rate drift up constantly. And it's true of long events. One of the issues in long events is muscle damage. Even at relatively low intensities, muscle fibres suffer damage, and over time you get less efficient. You consume the same oxygen and fuel, but you produce less power. If you want to keep the power output the same, you have to do it by recruiting a greater mass of muscle, which produces more damage, and so the cycle goes on.

So those neat physiological points, VO2 max, LT2, LT1, aren't static as regards power. They shift down. If you want to ride a long event at LT1, you're going to be riding less hard at the end in absolute terms than you were when you started. It's easy to assume that the drop in power is all about energy deficit or fatigue, but the changes in the landmarks of your basic physiology are also part of the problem.

'It's not about what you can do at the start,' said Mark Burnley. 'It's about what you can do hours later into the race. What can you sustain? But at least if LT1 is high to begin with, that will help. A bit.'

One academic study of a 24-hour race ridden by an experienced competitor found that by riding guided by perceived exertion, he started the race at 250 watts average for the first couple of hours, dropping to 150 watts by the end – a fall-off of 37%. If you compare that to the pacing you'd expect of a similarly experienced competitor on a shorter race (or, for that matter, the same rider in a shorter race), that sounds catastrophically bad.

Even Christoph Strasser, the most successful ultra rider of the last decade or so, saw a drop from 260 watts to 190 watts over the course of a 24-hour track record in 2017. In his defence, he reckoned it was one of the worst events he'd ridden – he had little track experience, and found the whole ride difficult.

(I have plenty of track experience – and I can think of almost nothing I'd want to do less than try to set a 24-hour track record. Even at fairly modest speeds, the G-forces on the banking make life deeply unpleasant, and the need to negotiate a curve every few seconds makes any attempt to check out mentally for a few moments quite impossible. I'd rather do 24 hours on an indoor trainer – but obviously that's not me actually volunteering.)

In a 24-hour race it seems that almost whatever you do there's an issue around about eight hours – assuming you're riding reasonably close to an LT1 target, despite almost whatever you do power seems to drop. It's not just power that changes. If heart rate in ultra riding obeyed the laws of nearly any other form of endurance exercise, you'd really expect it to keep going up. But at about eight hours, it invariably drops.

In the 24-hour race study I mentioned earlier, heart rate dropped from 140 bpm to 100 bpm as power dropped from 250 watts to 150 watts. Even if power stays more stable, heart rate still drops. When Christoph Strasser broke the road 24-hour record in 2021 his power stayed more consistent than is typical – it dropped from 280 watts to 240 watts over the ride. His heart rate still fell from 150 bpm to 120 bpm.

Since heart rate typically increases during a race because of things like heat stress and dehydration, one possible explanation would be that with very low effort levels and sweat rates, riders can drink enough to actually increase their level of hydration. The lack of heat stress took me by surprise in my first long events. You get very accustomed to the idea that racing is a hot activity, and you automatically dress accordingly. It's a shock a few hours into a 12- or 24-hour race to realize that you should have worn the sort of kit you'd wear for a slow-paced training ride. I spent most of one of my early 12-hour events freezing, and the cognitive dissonance was such that I couldn't work out why. The other factor that may affect heart rate is whether the rider's metabolism has switched to an increasingly fat-dominated fuelling – but that would also tend to reduce power, which confuses the issue. (We'll come back to why this would be the case when we're looking at nutrition in ultras.) And another possibility is that we need to look towards the interaction of physiology and psychology – the drop in heart rate might be the brain playing a role in this.

In longer, multi-day events, the physiology is not as predictable (or perhaps I mean 'even less predictable'), because other factors weigh more heavily. In a study done at the Race Across America (based on the ride of a two-man relay team) the authors found that power declined from a high on the first day, to a low in mid-race (around 1,500 km) and then started to rise again, finishing about 12% down on day one. That's not an uncommon pattern, but different riders can have very different experiences. Typically power output is higher during the day, by around 10%. All of this is roughly aligned with psychological questionnaires compiled during very long events – we'll come back to this later, but in general the most difficult bits are in the middle.

But when it comes to very long races, physiology is a small issue. The exercise physiologist Greg Whyte has ridden RAAM as part of a relay, as well as having a background as both a competitor and a coach in a very wide variety of ultra running and swimming events. He put it to me really simply. 'The pace is not fast. It's not hard to do 150 watts and ride at maybe 20 mph. What's hard is keeping doing it when you've had no sleep, when you're pissed off. Things will start to hurt, but only very rarely is it your legs that give up.'

*

I'm not the first person to wonder what would happen if they went on a very long bike ride. The bicycle was born into a world already obsessed with endurance, ultra endurance and the outer reaches of what you could endure. There was almost nothing the Victorians didn't want to explore the limits of.

The first bicycles didn't have pedals – they were like the sort of balance bike you give to a toddler, and the limit of endurance on one of those was firstly chafing, which since you were sitting astride a plank was justifiably legendary, and secondly patience, because on anything other than a perfect surface they were no faster than walking.

When someone put pedals on a bicycle (who it actually was remains something of a mystery) it all changed. In Paris, where bicycles with pedals were invented, they were initially viewed as a curiosity – riding a bike was a skill you would master for its own sake, like a skateboard trick. But when the first one made its way across the Channel to London, it was very quickly measured up for other possibilities.

The first long ride was performed by a Londoner called John Myall in 1868. He had bought one of the first half-dozen bicycles sold in Britain, and within a few weeks of learning to ride it, decided that instead of riding laps of a nice dry gymnasium, or trundling it round Hyde Park, he would ride it to Brighton. This was a ride of 50 miles or so, and had been established as a 'standard' challenge for wagers about how fast you could do it, by foot, by horse, or by carriage, since at least 1800.

It was November and the roads were already well into their winter state – rutted, muddy, unlit. It was the sort of challenge you set yourself based on at least 50% ignorance of reality. And he failed on the first attempt. But on his second attempt a few days later, knowing better what to expect, he made it to Brighton in just over 14 hours, at an average speed of about 4 mph, starting and finishing in pitch darkness.

This was probably the first ultra ride. Certainly it was the first thing that captured the spirit. Several other riders followed his lead – in the subsequent January three men rode from Liverpool to London over three days; not long after that there were rides from York and Bath. These routes took the roads used by the old mail coaches. By the 1860s, the coaches had long since been replaced by the railways, so the roads were almost abandoned – you could ride for miles and meet almost nothing other than the odd farm cart. Inevitably the challenge quickly came to be trying to beat the old mail coach times, which in due course begat a whole network of UK place-to-place records that you can still, should you feel like it, have a go at today. More often than not, the start and finish will still be a city's main Post Office or, at least as often, where the main Post Office used to be before it became a Wetherspoons pub.

In November 1869, almost exactly a year after Myall rode to Brighton, the first seedling of long distance racing appeared. It took the form of the Paris–Rouen race, 124 km or 77.5 miles. This was in an era when cycling was still trying to decide whether it was about racing or doing tricks, whether it was an indoor sport or an outdoor sport, whether women were allowed, what costume you wore to do it. The rules for Paris–Rouen were not extensive, but did include a ban on being pulled by dogs or using a sail, which captures some of the anarchic spirit. You could have two wheels, or three or four, or even one, and if you wanted to compete under an alias, that was fine too. First prize was 1,000 francs, which would be something around £10,000 today, which seems like a lot of money for something so chaotic.

It was won by James Moore, originally from Bury St Edmunds in England, in 10 hours 45 minutes. The first woman, Elizabeth Turner, arrived 12 hours later, edging out her husband for 29th place. The final finishers, 33rd and 34th of the 120 who set out, arrived a couple of hours after her, just over a day since leaving Paris.

This was still firmly in the adventuring phase of the whole game. In the UK and US, things got more serious quite quickly, because while cycling was new, endurance challenges were well established. Cycling followed in the footsteps of pedestrianism. There was a considerable history of foot racing, most often heel-and-toe walking, meaning that the toe of one foot couldn't leave the ground till the heel of the other foot had landed. It was driven by gambling, and often as not involved aristocrats setting their footmen against each other. Over time the challenges became increasingly eccentric, because obviously that makes the outcome much harder to predict, and the wager that much more interesting.

For instance, in 1809, noted long distance walker Captain Robert Barclay won a very famous bet that he could walk one mile in each of 1,000 consecutive hours – which adds up to 42 days. He completed this challenge on Newmarket Heath, and over the 42 days had attracted enough publicity that he walked his last few miles in front of thousands of spectators. This was in a pre-railway age when travelling to watch someone winning a bet was a bit more of an undertaking. Pedestrianism was a major sport.

By the time the bicycle arrived, one of the most established events on the pedestrian scene on both sides of the Atlantic was the six-day race. This was just what it sounds like. How far can you travel in six days? (Six days because you couldn't, or at least wouldn't, race on a Sunday.) Mostly still heel-and-toe, but also increasingly with classifications for go-as-you-please, which allowed running. The gradual change was simply because enforcing the heel-and-toe rule was difficult and exhausting for referees. With substantial money riding on events, things could get somewhat tense. The races were held indoors, on very small tracks, surrounded by spectators puffing on cigars and drinking till they fell over.

To put the challenge in some context, in 1882 George Littlewood walked 531 miles in six days in Sheffield, on a track that was 135 metres long, or 13 laps to the mile. That's 88.5 miles per day, 3.7 mph average, not allowing for breaks or sleep. In 1888, he covered 623 miles in a go-as-you-please race in New York. That record stood for 96 years. His walking one stands to this day.

This wasn't an amateur sport. Littlewood's major competitor was Charles Rowell of the US. In 1879, he won $50,000 over two races at a packed-out Madison Square Garden in New York.

Cycling dropped neatly into this exact format, beginning with David Stanton's 1878 wager that he could ride 1,000 miles in six days. At the Agricultural Hall in Islington, he banged out the 1,000 miles in just three. The following year the same venue hosted the Long Distance Championship of the World (since there was no governing body to accredit such a thing, this was pure marketing). This event was held on a 150-metre, unbanked, square track, which was elevated above the floor so that spectators could mill around below it. But six-day cycling still didn't garner as much interest as the walking events, and by the late 1870s even they were beginning to die off.

The six-day events only took off properly after export to the US, where they were a big hit at Madison Square Garden in the 1890s. They attracted huge crowds, complete with bands who would turn out in support of individual riders, and compete to drown each other out. Meanwhile on the track, riders rode themselves comatose, had frequent hallucinations, and regularly fell sound asleep from their bikes. New York's city fathers attempted to ban the races as an inhumane freak show. They did this by legislating that racers could only ride 12 hours a day. The race promoters' devious response was the Madison race, where both riders are on track all the time, but only one of them is 'racing', the other is lapping slowly round the top of the track ready to be relayed in.

In the middle of the night the racing wound down to a sort of truce, and the pairs might take it in turns to snatch some sleep. That version was still hugely popular, but wasn't really an ultra race in quite the same way. A modern six-day sees racing only in the evenings of the six days, which is a long way from riding a penny farthing for a week.

The real slog was moving outdoors. This was largely because of the invention of firstly the safety bicycle, and secondly the pneumatic tyre, that made long distance rides on rough roads much more achievable. In Northern Europe, the road classics began. The first was Liège–Bastogne–Liège, which started in 1892. At 250 km long, it was won in 10 hours 48 minutes by Léon Houa (who won in 1893 and 1894 as well). So, as far as duration was concerned, not far off the old Paris–Rouen. Liège–Bastogne–Liège was followed by other road races, including Paris–Roubaix in 1896, and the other one-day Monuments in the early twentieth century. But for the most part, while their distances stayed the same, the rapid speeding-up of pro road racing meant that their durations quickly became quite a lot shorter.

The first real, hardcore ultra race was, however, just around the corner. That, in 1903, was the Tour de France. Its conception was pure ultra – it was to be as gruelling a test as possible, designed to push athletes to their limits and hopefully beyond. The father of the race, Henri Desgrange, subsequently declared that his perfect race would be one so tough that only a single rider could finish.

The early Tours were a straightforward circumnavigation of France. The first one was 2,428 km, covered over 19 days in just six stages that averaged 405 km each. The longest stage was the final one, which was 471 km and took the winner (Maurice Garin, who won the event overall) more than 18 hours to complete. Some of the other riders came in hours behind him.

It got longer. The 1926 race was 5,745 km, in 17 stages – that year the number of stages was reduced because Desgrange thought that the previous year's 312-km stage average was too short, and the race was getting too easy. The longest stage the race ever saw was stage five in 1919. It was 482 km, and won in just under 19 hours. (All of the other stages that year were in the 14–15-hour range.)

Stages would start at midnight or in the early hours and continue into the following night. In the early editions officials didn't follow the racers, instead relying on checkpoints, both advertised and ambush, where they had to get a card stamped. There are stories about finish officials waiting outside a café by a stage finishing line having a brandy and waiting to see who would loom out of the night, and wondering if the answer might be 'no one'.

It didn't start out as a team event, and while teams quickly became accepted from a marketing and sponsorship point of view, a team's riders still weren't allowed to help each other on the road until 1913. Desgrange remained a fan of solo effort, to the extent of imposing a short-lived rule that if a rider could win a stage on their own by more than 20 minutes, they could have half of everyone else's prize money. If you didn't seem to be at least trying to win for yourself, you could be penalized or disqualified. If you sat on someone else's wheel for more than a few moments, you could be penalized or disqualified.

No outside help was permitted until 1930. Before that you had to fix your own bike, find your own food and drink, find the route on your own. It was the essence of an unsupported ultra event. When Eugene Christoph was famously penalized 10 minutes in 1913 for letting a boy work the bellows in a borrowed forge as he repaired his own forks, he'd already carried the broken bike for two hours down the Col du Tourmalet.

Nor was he the only one. Jean Alavoine, who won 17 stages between 1909 and 1923, once had his bike disintegrate below him just 10 km from the finish of the final stage and ran the rest of the way carrying the remains. Firmin Lambot, who won the Tour in 1922, always carried 500 francs in his jersey pocket so that he could buy a new bike if necessary. He was not an especially optimistic man.

The roads were rough, punctures were frequent – in the 1919 race, Jean Alavoine got 46 punctures, every single one of which he had to repair himself. Some of the mountain passes were little more than goat tracks, and if riders hadn't already been reduced to walking by the gradient, they'd quite possibly have been reduced to walking by the surface they were faced with riding over. Crashes on the way back down were frequent. The parcours has got a resonance with some of the gravel sections of the current Transcontinental Race.

So the Tour started out as a twenty-first-century ultra race, just 100 years before its time. In terms of format, it wasn't non-stop – there were a few snatched hours of sleep between stages, although for many riders some of that time was taken up trying to find somewhere to stay because the organizers didn't book anything. But otherwise it was long, it was brutal, it was designed to find the strongest not primarily by speed, but by body-breaking endurance. It made its fortune with stories of hardship and suffering. For the reports of *L'Auto*, the paper that employed Desgrange and sponsored the race, it was a story that rendered exaggeration almost obsolete. For their readers, there was the thrill of reading about something so gruesome yet so harmless. It was the perfect turn of the century event. If I had the backing, I'd run it again right now as unaltered as I could make it.

*

So what, then, of my first 24-hour race? Did my experience of that fit with what I'd come to expect? Power and heart rate? Heat and hydration?

The National 24 in 2023 was run in coolish and very, very wet conditions on a series of circuits in Shropshire, starting and finishing close to Wrexham. Riders set off one at a time between one and two o'clock in the afternoon. Mike and my helpers set up camp on a slight climb that was on three of the four circuits – if you're going uphill, it slows you down nicely for taking things from the team, because the rules mean they can only hand up stuff on foot, and not out of a car window. Depending what circuit I was on I'd see them every 80 minutes or every 40 (roughly – clearly it depended how fast I was going). On the night circuit – the 80-minute one – two of them formed a satellite team at the other end of the circuit.

After the race I could scroll through the team WhatsApp group chat and find endless conversations about me. 'Didn't take the bottle from us – make sure he takes one next time and tell him to drink it this time.' 'He looks like crap at the moment, but he's still going.' A lot of these conversations revolved around the colour coding we used for feeds and bottles, depending on their contents. So, 'Missed the double yellow, make sure he takes at least a single yellow or a green next time he passes you.' Things like that. The race can be just as involving for a support crew as for a rider, and the chat had the distinctive air of something that mattered like mad to the participants at the time but was forgotten the instant the race finished.

Mike was an excellent advisor. He's won the race several times and he's a teacher by profession, so maybe that's not a surprise. He worked out a rough schedule, aimed at riding around 500 miles and perhaps to a podium place, but he was also clear that this was only a guideline – we'd see what happened as the race unfolded. He scheduled two stops, one to put on warmer kit for the night section, and one in the morning after the air had warmed a little to take it off again. Each of these was to take four minutes, so I was going to be riding, all being well, for 23 hours 52 minutes.

We talked about the nutrition plan – the details of which we'll get back to later – and adapted some details of it just for practicality. We taped food bags to bottles, for instance, so there was only one thing to grab at a hand up rather than two. He told me about small things I wouldn't have thought out for myself, like the fact that the night circuit really only came into play at about 11 p.m. That meant that the final laps of the previous, much more twisty day circuit would happen in pitch darkness, so I needed to make sure I'd learned the course from the previous laps in daylight. Mike gave me a chance to start the race with a little bit of his experience to my credit.

All races are different, though. What was different about this one, even from Mike's previous events, was that it rained very heavily and without cessation for the first 13–14 hours, so through until around dawn on day two. There were flooded roads, and fairly regularly trucks would overtake me through puddles and drench me in cold, dirty water. And I mean proper gasping-for-breath and thinking-about-a-tetanus-shot sort of water. I was sodden for most of the event, and I can't emphasize how little of an issue heat stress was.

Hydration was only a problem in as much as I had to pee about once every two hours. It was hard to drink little enough given that most of the calories were coming in the form of energy drinks, and because of the weather barely any water was leaving me in sweat or condensation in my breath. This brings us to one of the more arresting messages of the many I received from Mike Broadwith in the weeks running up to the event. The opening few words that flashed up on my watch were, 'We need to talk about catheters...'

My feeling was very strongly that our need to talk about catheters was nil, so I ignored the rest of the message for several hours. When I did check it, I found a link to a supplier of external catheters – basically an adhesive condom with a tube and a bag. 'You don't need the bag,' said Mike. 'Just run the tube down your shorts, poke the end out when you need it, and try not to pee into your sock.'

With deep misgivings, I ordered a sample kit. As part of the service, a few days after it arrived, someone from the company rang me to see how it was going and offer advice. He was a bit surprised at the use I was putting their product to. Having thought about it for a moment, he added, 'Of course we sell quite a few to pilots and bell-ringers, so I suppose why not?' and that's a Venn diagram I never expected to be a part of. But Mike was right, it was a lot faster than stopping and a lot nicer than just peeing into your shorts – which is a fairly common approach. I still never mastered peeing and pedalling at the same time, and the feeling was not a pleasant one, but if I'd had to stop, I'd have tripled or quadrupled my stopped time for the race.

As to power, well, that dropped all right. I started out with what felt like a fairly conservative target power – on the basis that my LT1 was in the region of 290 watts I made that my never-exceed power, and aimed for 250 watts or thereabouts as the steady state. I managed to stick relatively close to that for the early parts of the race. The average power was 249 watts for the first three hours. Generally, that meant seeing 250 watts or thereabouts on the computer on the flat, 290 watts on the climbs, and ideally zero on any sort of descent that was steep enough to keep the speed over 20 mph. The cadence was nice and low, because at low powers that's more efficient. Ultra marathon runners typically develop a sort of shuffle, where the stride length is modest and their feet never get very far off the ground, and a cadence of maybe 85 rpm (I'd typically race a short distance event at somewhere between 100 and 105 rpm) is the bike-riding equivalent.

Heart rate for the same block averaged 138 bpm, with a maximum of 162 bpm (and trust me, that was a short-lived mistake in the first few minutes). This was very, very easy. It wasn't fun, because there were substantial periods when the rain was so heavy it was difficult to see, and after a while the puddles meant you couldn't tell where the edge of the road was. But physically it wasn't hard to do – it was an easy training pace.

If I scroll on through the file uploaded from my bike computer to 8–12 hours, power dropped to 211 watts. Heart rate dropped to 124 bpm, which is not actually all that much. If you look at the ratio of power to heart rate, it's not far out of line with the power drop. Cadence stayed around the same; the average dropped a little, to 80 rpm, but mainly because that section of the course was hillier, and that meant steady cadence on the way up, and free-wheeling on the way down. I'd be lying if I didn't admit that even 10 hours in, the next opportunity to stop pedalling and have a bit of a stretch was never far from my thoughts.

Unfortunately the next few hours of the ride weren't recorded, because the unremitting rain and spray finally outsmarted my electronics, and I wasn't back online until

15 hours. That meant 2 a.m. till 5 a.m. are unrecorded, and so, by the logic of modern cycling, didn't actually happen. But don't worry, I can remember them. Vividly.

It's a pity not to have the data. Relative to the opposition, it was my fastest segment of the race. Through the hours of darkness and pouring rain I went from fourth place to second. This was, I think, a pacing error. I'm good at pacing short rides on instinct and experience, but long rides as a novice are much more difficult. I'm pretty sure that in the absence of any data to guide me, I just went too hard. The problem was that with the effort levels so moderate, and the night so wet and miserable, I gradually got a little cold, and the instinctive solution to that was to ride a bit harder to generate some heat. It wasn't a conscious decision, and the overreach was probably only a few watts, but in terms of pacing the overall ride things were always quite finely balanced.

It was an easy mistake to make. There aren't a lot of external cues for guidance in the middle of the night. I caught other riders consistently, but with the spread of speeds people were going at, that was almost a given. I didn't have anything as quaint as a pacing plan working off turns and landmarks, and even if I had, I didn't have any means of telling the time more accurately than the sunrise. It was significant, I think, that a couple of hours after that, with the temperature going back up and the sun finally out, I was still cold.

When I got the computer back at 5 a.m., things had gone south. From 18 hours till 21 hours, power averaged 170 watts, heart rate 111 bpm. The final three hours were

150 watts and 107 bpm. It could have been worse, but it could have been a lot better too – it's in line with some other rides by experienced riders, but it's a much bigger fall-off than you'd be looking for if you were, let's say, Christoph Strasser or Mike Broadwith.

The final few hours were round a small finishing circuit of about 8 miles on an industrial estate outside Wrexham. I have an unpleasantly vivid memory of riding over a bumpy section of road that had clearly been much used by heavy lorries, in a full-on time trial position with the skinsuit, the helmet and all the trimmings, and putting out a feeble 100 watts. At that point in my day that was all I could do. When Mike started encouraging me to catch the rider ahead of me in the standings he shouted, 'Come on! He's only a mile up on you! Light the afterburners!' I remember thinking, 'Mike, the afterburners are as lit as they're ever going to be. This is it. I'm giving you whatever I still have.' It was comical, and I mean literally comical. I laughed out loud, which is the sort of thing that makes people think you're having fun.

So, overall, my own experience wasn't all that far off what passes for normal in the world of a 24-hour race. I was a bit weaker at the end than a more experienced, or maybe just durable, rival would have been. In those last few hours I slipped from the second place I'd been in at dawn to a final placing of fourth by the time my race ran out at about 2 p.m. A bit slower overnight, especially in the hours immediately before dawn, and I might have gone further. Or, if I hadn't gone further, I might at least have had a nicer time.

The distance I covered was 486.63 miles. That's just over 20 mph, with an average power of 209 watts, and a total calorie burn of 14,000 kcal. It was, I reckoned, not bad for a first go.

4

Very Long Rides Don't Make You Fast, They Just Make You Tired

For over a decade of my life, from my mid-twenties to late-ish thirties, training was essentially what I did for a living. While I had other things to do, training was almost every day's primary objective. Everything else fitted around it, and if it didn't fit, it didn't happen. It wasn't a normal job. Even if you're quite deeply entrenched in that world, you don't get to the point where you think spending four hours a day cycling and two hours every afternoon napping in an altitude simulation tent is normal – although I'd like to say that if you've never done this, you're missing out.

So I know quite a lot about it, I know how to do it, and I know how it works. It works simply by creating a stimulus that leads to an adaptation. Your body normally exists in a rough equilibrium or homeostasis, one that is adapted to the demands you put on yourself. If you're sedentary, this equilibrium will reflect that. If you're active, it will reflect that. To be wildly simplistic, you are what you do. What you can achieve with specific training is a more dramatic adaptation, one that isn't necessarily reflective of a normal life, but one that is devoted to a specific set of probably rather artificial demands – lifting very heavy weights, running 100 metres in under 10 seconds, or perhaps riding a bike very quickly or for an unreasonably long period of time.

Almost all of what we're interested in in ultra riding is aerobic fitness. There is not very much use for specifically anaerobic (sprint) ability. Even then, the demands of ultra riding are so diverse that looking at just the physiology of energy transfer is only ever going to be part of the story – it tells you nothing about how your neck is going to feel after two days, or how to deal with weird points of failure like the discovery 22 hours into a 24-hour time trial championship that the muscles I use to raise my eyebrows would fail so that I could no longer look upwards as I needed to do to see where I was going when I had my head in a low aerodynamic position. I didn't even know that was possible. They didn't hurt, they just didn't work – I'd try to raise my eyebrows and nothing would happen. I've never even heard of such a thing. But all the same, aerobic fitness is as good a place to start as any.

The perception is that training is a long slow process – and it certainly feels like it. But it's interesting that some changes actually happen very fast, at least at a biochemical level. As already mentioned, physical movement depends on some chemistry, namely the continuous production of ATP. This molecule is produced in the cells using fat and carbohydrate and ideally some oxygen as the key starting point. Assuming you have enough of these available, the reaction depends on cell structures called mitochondria, and a variety of associated enzymes.

These enzyme levels can increase very quickly – the level of aerobic enzymes in muscle can double in five to ten days of training, which you'll notice from a very clear improvement in fitness. The number and size of the mitochondria increase in just a few weeks, which also has a significant impact.

Blood volume is also something that is changed by exercise, and again is something that will increase quickly. You can actually measure an increase in blood volume within 24 hours of a first training session, and total volume might increase by as much as 20% after just three to six training sessions – probably less than 10 days. Given blood's central role in moving oxygen around the body, it's not surprising that this has a positive effect on aerobic performance.

This is the case regardless of the fact that most of this early change is in plasma volume, not the red cells or haemoglobin that actually carry the oxygen. As a bonus it will increase your heat tolerance and your ability to deal with dehydration.

Your ability to use fat as a fuel at a sub-maximal ('steady') pace will improve quite quickly as well – and if you think about the demands of an ultra event, you'll see that that is a very useful thing. You can be a much better athlete in less than a month, and I think coaches should mention this more often. If you've got a long ride in two weeks that you've somehow never got around to training for, it is not too late to get a few sessions in.

However, one normally takes longer over it. The adaptations that start to happen quickly will keep happening. And there are other adaptations that are not as fast to kick in. Changes in blood vessels – especially an increase in the number of the tiny capillaries that deliver blood into the depths of the muscle – take longer. The heart will get bigger, its walls will get thicker, it will pump more blood with each beat – perhaps as much as 60% more than a sedentary person. This is not an adaptation that happens especially fast; the 'athlete's heart' is something that is seen most clearly after years of training at an elite level.

Longer term training also has benefits on your pulmonary system – your lungs, essentially. Mainly, at a sub-maximal level, it increases the efficiency of your lungs. There's less energy cost to the basic act of breathing, and that leaves more oxygen available for all the other muscles.

Historically most of the interest in all of this has centred on what I used to do – short, hard efforts over relatively short time frames from a few minutes to a few hours. In something like a 40-km time trial, taking maybe 45 minutes, the limits to performance are all about how much oxygen you can move. A talented, well-trained rider can sustain maybe 90% of their absolute maximum oxygen shifting ability.

So the question then is what does it mean for a long race, where the level you need to sustain is a lot lower? As I said in the previous chapter, the idea in a long race is to sit below LT1, the first point at which blood lactate levels start to drift up. In lab tests, for me that was always somewhere between 60% and 65% of my maximum aerobic capacity – it's a nice sustainable pace. It's not a tremendous athletic feat, at least not in the short term.

Only after I'd planned for, trained for and ridden my first 24-hour race did I go and look at the website of the 24 Hour Fellowship in the UK – an association for riders of the 24-hour. They offer a sample training programme. It's brutal. It's made clear that it was the training of an elite 24-hour rider (someone they describe as a 'super champion') rather than an entry-level programme, but it's brutal all the same. It starts with a winter of unspecified easy cycling, and some heavy weights in the gym, focusing on bench press, trunk curl and power clean.

Then at Easter it moves onto the road, and how. Thirty-five miles five mornings a week, as hard as sustainable, followed by a 10–15-mile commute home from work and a further 15–30 miles in the evening, so three rides a day. Saturday morning, 50–70 miles. Sunday morning, 130 miles possibly including a race. This is simply huge training – it's up to 600 miles a week, at least 175 miles of it at a full-on pace, and with no rest days. It would take over 30 hours and isn't far off the volume of a full Tour de France repeated end to end for three to four months. I honestly don't know how anyone did that, but clearly if they did and they survived, a 24-hour time trial would be fairly easy.

That would probably have killed me, and I'm not speaking figuratively. That would have been just about my biggest week as a pro repeated and repeated, and there's no way that at the end of it I'd be fit for anything, let alone a bike race. If I'd seen this training programme before my own rides, I might have decided that the ultra riders could have ultra riding and I'd do something else. Happily I didn't, so I was free to try to work out how to train for an ultra without the fear that I was coming in short by 400 miles a week hanging over me.

The key thing about training is that it is specific. This might be the single most important thing to know about it. The training is determined by the event target. As both a rider and a coach I've tried to break down the demands of an event, and find ways to stimulate appropriate adaptations. Even if a major target event was a time trial of a fairly standard distance, so already very much my thing, if it was hillier than usual I'd look for ways to recreate the demands of the hills. That might involve riding efforts at higher torques to recreate the way you have less momentum on a climb. And, because the physics of riding a hilly race mean that the fastest approach is to ride harder on the hills and back off on the descents, I'd do training repeats over and under my average race pace to train the ability to ride harder on the climbs and then recover on the descents.

Riders training for races like the Tour de France will take it further, and look for roads that simulate the right gradients, at the right altitudes, of key stages of that year's race. They ride sessions to recreate the possible scenarios of the race, from a physical point of view – following an attack, sustaining an attack. The coaches monitor fitness not just as an overall, generalized thing, but their riders' fitness for very specific tasks.

So the alarming logic of specificity is that training for a very long bike race would consist mainly of, well, very long bike rides. If you want to ride for 24 hours, my first instinct would be that the training rides should regularly hit 8–12 hours, with possibly a few longer ones thrown in. If you want to do a two-week race, it could be even more demanding. That 600-mile week starts to shimmer into view.

But training has diminishing returns, and in my experience they set in long before 600 miles a week. There are very good practical reasons for not wanting to spend too much of one's life doing 12–24-hour training rides – namely sustaining a job or a relationship, keeping your energy-drink budget under control and maybe retaining at least some skin on your rear end. Above all, there is a competing principle of training, which is consistency. You need to keep doing it. You create a training stimulus by some physical effort or another. You then have to recover from that, which gives your body a chance to refuel, rehydrate (if necessary) and, more important, adapt.

The mechanism by which adaptation happens isn't totally straightforward. Some of it is hormonal, for example. Hormones released as a response to exercise stimulate the upregulation of certain genes, which prompts the production of proteins to alter your physiology. A nice classic example is the hormone EPO (erythropoietin), with which anyone following pro cycling over the last couple of decades will be familiar. It's produced in response to the stimulation of reduced oxygen availability at altitude, and it upregulates a gene that leads to the production of haemoglobin to make the blood better at transporting oxygen. (The benefits of introducing EPO artificially in contravention of the doping rules are pretty obvious – it is phenomenally effective.)

All of this takes time, and it takes energy. It works best if the stimulus is fairly regular, with adequate recovery between sessions. Excessive fatigue is counterproductive – your body is so overwhelmed that you don't see the medium- and long-term adaptation. Several riders I spoke to said simply that 'Very long rides just make you tired. They don't make you fit.' And that's because if you do them often enough to keep creating the stimulus, you can't recover and adapt. If you do them with enough recovery between them, the stimuli are too far apart.

There's also the question of exactly what I mean by specificity. Because you can look at it two ways. Are we talking about the event itself, or about the physiology needed for the event? In a 'normal' race, these are close together. If you want to develop a high LT2, good economy and good fat burning for a four- to six-hour pro road race, a good basis of the training is four- to six-hour rides, with some shorter, harder efforts either mid-ride, or structured into other, shorter days. The physiological stimulus and the event format point towards the same general area.

For a much longer event, 24-hour to a couple of weeks, probably the main target is LT1. And the best way to train LT1 isn't to spend 12 hours bumbling round the countryside very slowly. Instead, you'd probably look to shorter, slightly harder efforts, probably working off a base of intensity just under your existing LT1, with some harder steady efforts above it. This is, in fact, the basis of 'normal' training for most pro riders. The properly traditional way to train is to put in a winter and early spring of high volume, moderate intensity riding just like this before swapping in some harder, shorter efforts and more specialized sessions as the target events of the season approach. The intuitive way to look at it is that you're building a base, and only after you have a solid base should you start putting anything on top of it.

This is far from the only way to do it. You can do base work with intensity thrown in from the start, or you can even reverse the whole plan and do the hard bits first and the steady bits later, but the concept of a base is still familiar. When I did these things seriously, the base phase started in January and lasted into sometime in March. I did lots of rides in the three- to four-hour bracket, with increasing duration efforts at just under LT2 – maybe 40 minutes, maybe even an hour on a big day. The aim was ultimately to hit 30–40% of my time over LT1 by the point at which that phase of training came to an end. And the most notable physiological effect of that regime was that LT1 went up, significantly.

Looking back at a training log from my last pro year, in eight weeks LT1 increased from 285 watts to 335 watts. (This was a year when I'd been ill for several weeks before starting training, so my baseline numbers were a little lower than normal.) LT2 barely moved during this period, so that I was in the odd position of LT1 being only about 30 watts lower than LT2 – later in the year, with more specific training, the difference would be more like 70 watts. This pattern was entirely normal for me. What I was doing, had I but known it, was training myself as an ultra rider.

It worked all right for my 12-hour races – there were plenty of mistakes in the first couple of those, but they were in execution rather than in training. I rolled into those off 'normal' fitness, for 'normal' races – the race targets for those seasons were mostly 20–60-minute events. I had no complaints about my physical condition, and in fact for the third 12-hour I did, the one where I got it right, I'd have said my fitness was perfectly well matched to the race.

Mike Broadwith, when I asked him what he did, said he simply commuted to work and back. 'It's about 90 minutes each way,' he told me. 'So that's a very easy way to get three hours a day of riding done.' From my own point of view heading towards a 24-hour, that was a reassuring reality check.

He's not the only one with that approach. Ian Walker broke the record for riding between the northernmost and southernmost points of Europe, something he did in 2018. It's a ride of 6,367 km, which he did in just under 17 days. He's also been a Transcontinental Race rider. In his day job he's a professor of environmental psychology, and the author of a justifiably famous paper that investigated the amount of space overtaking drivers give to cyclists, and which found that he was given appreciably more respect by drivers if he didn't wear a helmet, and even more if he wore a long blonde wig. His basic training regime was almost exactly the same as Broadwith's – he's a commuter. Given the largely amateur nature of the sport it probably shouldn't be a surprise.

There is a bonus to the commute. 'The commute is the backbone of it,' Walker told me. 'That's three hours a day, then I'd do a longer ride at the weekend. The commute has the big advantage that at the end of the day you don't want to do it – it might be raining, snowing, windy, cold, you might have had a bad day at work. But you have to, you have to get home or you're staying at work overnight. You learn to suck it up and that's not a bad thing. Doing that routinely helps.' Riding when you don't want to is a key skill, and not one that's easy to train.

In the same vein, Emily Chappell, a Transcontinental winner in 2016, started out her cycling career as a cycle courier in London. 'I just got used to being on the bike,' she said. 'It's stop start, but you're doing it all day, you don't really get to think about it, it's just your job. You get used to fuelling it whatever way you can, you get used to it.'

Emily is one of my favourite people in cycling, in equal measures adventurer and athlete. When she won in 2016 the media was fascinated by the idea of a cycle courier being good at cycling, as if it was the most unexpected association. At the time it seemed to me fairly natural. Training consists of not just the last few months, but of a whole history. Your economy as a rider keeps improving for years, which is obviously an asset for a long race. And you get that by just riding. In some ways couriering looks perfect. It's not the exhausting steady grind of doing something like an eight-hour endurance ride, but it's on and off, there's a bit of variety to the effort level, and above all it's hitting some decent training volume at the right sort of intensity. And, like a commute, you'll do it in all weathers, in all moods. Emily the courier to Emily the TCR winner makes complete sense.

There are one or two other considerations. There is the question of what your body uses as fuel. You want to burn as much fat as possible, and consequently keep the amount of carbohydrate you're using low, because carbohydrate is in much more limited supply. Longer training rides may help improve your fat burning – as a rule, fat utilization increases over the duration of a ride. That means there may still be a benefit to a longer ride, maybe once a week, assuming the associated fatigue doesn't interfere with the rest of the programme. It can be low in intensity, so ideally suited to a social ride. (And Emily's long days in the saddle might also be quite good from this point of view.)

You can try to take a shortcut on this by doing shorter rides in a fully fasted state. Typically done first thing in the morning after a protein-only breakfast, and with no energy taken on board during the ride. This can offer three of the most miserable hours of your life if you hit the ride even marginally too hard. Or you can do something very similar, but with a little carbohydrate and some protein coming in. This approach is a bit safer, in that one of the things you start doing if you ride in a very low carbohydrate condition is burn protein as well as fat. A little protein intake hopefully saves you from burning actual muscle.

The idea is that the relative absence of carbohydrate prompts fat burning. But it's not clear if it works. Physiologist Mark Burnley described it to me as a mixed issue. 'Maybe they work. Or maybe doing low carbohydrate rides just gives you a crap training session.' Certainly the intensity of a fasted ride is low. Anything more and you have a proper, hallucinogenic running-out-of-energy experience (the 'bonk').

VERY LONG RIDES DON'T MAKE YOU FAST

Although, that leads somewhere else. Ian Walker said that one of the skills needed was the ability to deal with the moment that you run out of everything and you're a) bereft of anything with calories in it, and b) many miles from the nearest Snickers bar. 'There's a technique to it. You can keep the pedals going round, sort of, even when you're long past having anything much left. You don't go fast, but you don't stop.' Is it something you want to rehearse? It won't be fun, it probably won't do much for you when things are going well, but it might do something for you when things are one day going very, very badly.

The most matter-of-fact rider I think I spoke to about riding very long events was also probably the best. Certainly over the last decade or so Christoph Strasser has won more than everyone else. He's a very straightforward 42-year-old Austrian, one of the few ultra riders who has analysed the events in the same way short distance riders do. He gives the slight impression that he can't understand why the rest of the cycling world isn't as good at this stuff as he is. I talked to him about a great many of the elements of ultra riding, and his method of breaking things down invariably made it sound very simple indeed.

And so it is with training. 'Training very long makes you very tired and it makes you slow,' he told me. 'You can do a 400- or 500-km training ride, but it takes too long to recover from it.'

His approach is what you'd expect of a shorter distance rider. 'My coach and I break it down into the numbers we want – FTP [functional threshold power], VO2 max – and we work our way towards seeing that.'

And what does Strasser's training look like in practice? 'I do a lot of interval-type training. Twenty seconds all-out, 40 seconds easy – maybe 30 repeats in a session. Four-minute or eight-minute all-out efforts, maybe 110% of FTP. Lots of sweet-spot intervals, done just below FTP, for 15, 20 or 30 minutes. At the start of the year it's actually quite intense – as the season gets going the rides tend to get a bit longer.' For anyone arriving from shorter distance racing, this is 'normal' training. The only variation is the idea of reducing the intensity and upping the volume a bit as the season progresses, but even that is normal enough that it's something I have tried a few times when preparing for target races of 20 minutes or so.

So there's a pattern here – long races don't demand long training. However, there's a but, and it arrives in the shape of Fiona Kolbinger. Kolbinger won the TCR overall in 2019, the first time that a woman had won the overall title at that level of event. She's an amateur, and works as a medical doctor, based in Dresden. Despite being a rider at a similar level to Strasser, she does things differently. For her, riding is very much secondary to her day job as a surgeon. She's an amateur in the traditional sense. She doesn't even do many interviews about her racing because (I think) for her that's not what it's about. Races are for doing, not for talking about.

Since there's not a lot of daylight left outside working hours in winter, she tends not to do all that much riding over the winter at all. She told me, 'I run, maybe some cross country skiing. Then in spring I do some distance: 200- and 300-km rides on back-to-back days – I like these long days on the bike.'

VERY LONG RIDES DON'T MAKE YOU FAST

Kolbinger had a different arrival in long distance riding from most competitors – shortly after buying a new bike when she was a medical student, she decided to ride to Helsinki, where her boyfriend was studying. 'It was 1,700 km,' she said. 'It took 12 days, 150 km a day. That was really the first thing I did with my bike. I didn't really train for it, I just did it. I just think I have a good body for long rides.'

Her approach since still prioritizes distance. When she moved to Dresden, she found a group of long distance riders based there, called the ElbSpitze. They run an annual race of around 700 km, south into the Alps – with quite a lot of climbing. It runs as a group ride for a lot of the way, with the climbs contested hard and a flat-out finale of over 100 km. That's a hard way to race. And to prepare for that, they organized a progressive series of very long training rides, 200 km, 250 km, 300 km, 350 km and 400 km, with more and more climbing in the route – 5,000–6,000 metres. 'It's hard training – it's mostly male riders, so it's really good for me. In the race they have food every 100–150 km, so you end up stopping, cooling right down, then having to get going again. For something like TCR it's good.'

In fact, for something self-supported like TCR, it's almost a rehearsal. It's a rather different answer to the question about whether training specificity for ultra riding means training for the physiology or training for the event compared to most other riders and coaches.

There is something that Christoph Strasser told me that I haven't mentioned yet. He did indeed say that very long rides make you tired, they don't make you fast. But he also said, 'Once you have experience, long rides are not necessary. I know what it's like.' He knew how he'd feel on the saddle after two or three days, he knew what his neck and shoulders would feel like, what emotions he'd be dealing with. 'I have done many, many long races. I know about my nutrition, what foods will work for me. I know how the sleep deprivation will affect me. I have tested my lighting system, I can see how different temperatures through the day and night affect me. You need this experience. But once you have it, you do not need to get it again.' When he set the 24-hour track record, he said he found that much harder than he'd been ready for, precisely because track experience was something he lacked. He'd expected it to be more like a road ride than it turned out to be.

One of the problems with asking experienced riders about preparing for any race is that they tell you what they do, not what they know. In a short time trial, perhaps there is not much to know, or much benefit to be had from experience – short time trials are about power and aerodynamics, not decision making. But the longer a race gets, the more complicated it becomes. There's probably some sort of geometric progression in operation – maybe a race twice the length offers four times the potential problems. Certainly my experience of 12-hour racing showed there were a lot more elements to balance and issues to cope with than there were in even something like a 100-mile race.

So ideally what you want to do is train specifically for two different things. Which you obviously can't do.

As was to be the case with a great deal of what I did to prepare for my 24-hour, I asked Mike Broadwith. I appointed

VERY LONG RIDES DON'T MAKE YOU FAST

him my guru, though I didn't make the mistake of telling him that.

The compromise we came up with was to train as if for a shorter event, in the way most of the ultra riders did (with the admittedly troubling exception of Fiona Kolbinger), but to throw in a couple of longer rides as well. If I did those as rehearsals of the race, so ridden at an LT1-ish sort of pace, in a racing position and on race kit, they'd fulfil a number of purposes.

I wasn't necessarily all that keen on this, because of the sheer fatigue of them and the necessary recovery – I agreed with Christoph Strasser that from a physical point of view there's not really a good way to do that sort of ride. But there were things I needed to know. I'd get an idea of whether my position on the bike was sustainable. If something was beginning to niggle after six hours, I was clearly going to know an awful lot more about it come 18 or 20 hours. I'd try, as hard as I could, to keep in that aerodynamic time trial position for as much of the long rides as I could. This isn't always easy to do outside a race, because on a normal ride there are junctions, villages, roundabouts – places where you have to get out of position to be safe. I could have done my six hours up and down the local trunk road between two roundabouts 10 miles apart, but even for someone who devoted a career to time trialling, there are limits.

The long rides would give me a chance to trial the first quarter of the race's nutritional strategy. This was probably my biggest concern. I once joked in a magazine column that ultra races were 'inconveniently mobile eating competitions', a comment made from the standpoint of knowing next to nothing about them, but which was repeated back to me approvingly by several ultra riders who had forgotten where it came from. Nutrition is a major element of any bike race longer than about an hour. Your target power is closely related to the physiological marker LT1, but how long you can sustain that for depends on fuelling – and we'll come back to this at some length later.

For the moment the question is just about two aspects of eating – the practicality and the palatability. The practicality is essentially a) can I carry it? b) can I unwrap it? c) can I eat it? Will it melt? Does it come in the sort of wrapper that is designed to frustrate both toddlers and tired bike riders? (These are quite similar states of being, incidentally.) Does it suck all the moisture from my mouth on contact and prove impossible to chew and swallow? These things aren't constants. The longer the ride, the less tolerant you get, in every sense. The palatability is what it tastes like after several hours, because this is something that can change as you fatigue.

Broadwith was also moderately insistent that at least one of these rides should finish after midnight. Firstly so that I would get a chance to ride at race speeds with lights – 'Go and ride somewhere really dark,' he said, 'and find some roads you don't know all that well.' And secondly because the sensation of the sun going down on a summer evening and the temperature dropping isn't one you're generally familiar with unless you've got previous experience with the very long bike ride.

I'll admit that six hours is not really very long – pro riders will do plenty of six-hour rides in a season. I'd like to point out that they don't generally do them in a time trial position, or completely non-stop, or with a real consistency of effort. They're more often than not a bit on the social side. One pro in Andorra used to suggest six-hour rides with other pros so he'd have plenty of time to try to persuade them to invest in his venture capital business. But all the same, six hours isn't all that hard.

But as a compromise it felt pitched about right. Long enough to find things out, not so long that it would take a week to recover from. And I did indeed find things out. On the first one, just around some of my local roads in a couple of three-hour laps, the saddle was very significantly uncomfortable by the end, in a way that worried me – I reckoned I could have managed another six hours or so, but beyond that was going to be unpleasant. It led to a couple of weeks of saddle-angle tweaking that got to the point that I bought a proper inclinometer to measure it to a tenth of a degree. (I was later to issue this inclinometer to my support team at the 24 with instructions to measure a suitable bit of ground for checking the angle of my saddle at any stops. They totally ignored this instruction, and fair enough, I'd have done the same. What can I say? I went a bit Mariah Carey.)

On the second ride, the saddle was fine but my lower back was not. This was the result of having angled the saddle nose down by about 3 degrees from its original level position. I put it back to 2.5 degrees afterwards, on the basis that either both saddle and lower back would be fine, or the compromise would mean they'd both hurt and maybe one would take my mind off the other and vice versa. But it showed the value of the longer in-position ride – my back was completely fine in three- to four-hour training rides on the same bike, to the point where I was liberally congratulating myself on the comfort of my set up. It was only the stress-test long ride that showed the problem, and it was a problem that would have ended my race.

Other things I learned: on the first ride I got knocked off by a van, which was an interesting lesson in mission blindness, because I just bounced up and got going again. I landed on a soft verge, and no real damage was done to me or the bike or the van. It was two days later before I even remembered it had happened. The total lack of consequence meant it was an oddly cheery encounter – the driver even said goodbye with a merry 'It was really nice to meet you!' which I have to admit I quite liked, even if the whole thing was his fault.

Nutrition was also all right – but even when I was doing it I reckoned that I'd have to be getting it very badly wrong to not last six hours at sub-LT1 pace. I had some solid food options to test, and the most useful thing I did was check I could unwrap them easily and eat them without dropping them. (It's amazing how many sports nutrition companies supply products in wrapping that would defeat you if you were standing in your kitchen at home. Although none of them equals the time in a 12-hour when I passed through an official feed zone organized by the race and accepted an anonymous paper bag, mainly because it was being proffered by a keen-looking 12-year-old and I didn't want to disappoint him. It contained an unpeeled orange.)

My lights worked as planned, too, on the sunset ride. I've trained at night a fair bit over the years, and my experience has generally been that there's a lot less traffic and it gives you quite a wide berth, so there wasn't really anything to alarm me in that. Potholes were the worst of it – I noticed it was sore on my neck having to look for details of road surface in the few seconds-worth of illumination I had available. But the chill of the evening was fine, and I was happy with the idea of racing all night.

Apart from the sore back, the worst of the long rides was getting a puncture at midnight, only about 5 miles from home, and having to fix it using my lights to see what I was doing. It turned out that this scenario was Glastonbury for small flying insects. When I changed the tube I put in a few weeks later, it was covered in tiny corpses, for whom I felt no sympathy at all.

Other than the long ones, my preparation for the 24-hour was normal training. Or rather, it would have been normal training if there had been about twice as much of it, and if I'd started doing it more than eight weeks before the race. When I took riding seriously most proper weeks were 16–20 hours; this time out my longest week (excluding the two with the six-hour rides) was about 12 hours. But it was the same sessions, over a lot of the same roads, and I did get a bit fitter. I certainly got more durable, which was probably more important.

A typical week had three 'long' rides – around three hours, usually with a 40-minute effort around LT2, so significantly over planned race pace. There would be another two days with an interval session, usually on the Zwift platform – a lot like the sessions Christoph Strasser talked about. The main benefit of the shorter efforts is with the muscles. They tend to press the same buttons that you press when you first start training. They affect the mitochondria, they increase the amount of enzyme in the muscle, and they can be quite a potent form of training.

Considering the specific target is LT1, there was quite a large proportion of riding that was above it. As a proportion it was probably a bit too much – but what was missing from the programme was volume. The riding that I left out when I cut things back was the steady stuff – those three-hour rides should probably have been four-hour rides, with the extra hour sub-LT1. And the frankly last-minute (eight weeks or so) decision to commit to the event produced what we might think of as training-insufficiency anxiety. The usual response to that, even for a very long event, is to hit the 'quality' button harder and more often.

The other thing that I threw into the mix was heat-tolerance training. The most obvious reason to do this was the possibility of it being a very hot event. It's more of an issue for races like RAAM, where the first few days are crossing an honest-to-God desert, and the daytime temperatures can be very high indeed. For that, heat conditioning is almost an essential. It increases sweat rate and improves cooling by conditioning your system to direct more blood to the skin. It can also reduce your heart rate in hot conditions. And it also just makes you used to exercising in the heat. I raced at the 2010 Delhi Commonwealth Games at midday in temperatures of almost 40 degrees, and having done some heat conditioning beforehand made it hot but not unbearable. My power output was lower than it would have been on a spring day in the UK, but I was still racing and in control.

Shropshire in July has hyperthermia as a fairly low risk factor. There are many witnesses prepared to testify to this. There have been one or two hot 24s in recent years, but generally it's tolerable, especially since it's usually cool overnight. The main reason for heat conditioning wasn't really to protect against the chances of a hot day. There's some recent evidence to suggest training in the heat has very happy effects on your performance in more normal temperatures. For example, it seems to increase blood plasma volume for a lot of athletes, which has a physiologically well-mapped-out cool weather benefit. It's a bit like altitude training – the adaptations you make to deal with an extreme environmental stress have benefits across the board.

While its effectiveness as a general concept is still somewhat up for debate, and it's effectiveness for any individual (in this case, me) is doubly uncertain, I decided to include it anyway. It had the attraction that it doesn't take all that long to do a session, but it still creates enough physiological stress to constitute a day's training. And there is an additional attraction in that most of the studies that support it also suggest that a very small number of sessions is required in total – perhaps as few as four, spaced maybe a week apart.

The session itself was short and horrible. I remembered heat conditioning being horrendous, but the sheer depth of it slips through your memory when you try to recall it. The protocol is not complicated – you ride in a temperature hot enough to increase your core body temperature. For me, this time, that meant a home trainer in my gym at home, with two fan heaters and a boiling wallpaper stripper jetting steam to get the humidity up. Generally I trained at about

35–37 degrees, 75–80% humidity. I didn't use a fan. I just sat there sweating like a grotesque water-feature.

My heart rate climbed as my power went down. I started the first session at a breezy 280 watts, and a heart rate of 140 bpm. Forty-five minutes later, while those numbers hadn't quite reversed, it felt like they had. The file shows my last five minutes had a power of 200 watts and a heart rate of 170 bpm. And that was a hard-fought 200 watts.

That part of the training was familiar. This time there was an added element, suggested by my former coach, the physiologist Jamie Pringle. 'Have a hot bath afterwards,' he said. 'Don't make it boiling hot, but make sure it's above body temperature.' The logic of this bit of sadism was to prolong the heat stimulus for no extra effort. Let me tell you, the bath was much more unpleasant than the bike riding. Sitting there, so hot, so unable to cool down, was just awful. At least on the bike you felt you had some control over what you were doing. In a hot bath I was basically a lobster. I've done some dreadful things to myself over the years, but this was hands down the worst. I highly recommend it if you're the sort of athlete who equates misery with achievement.

(If you do try it, by the way, be careful. Take the first session or two a bit cooler and shorter, till you've established what you're doing, and don't do it if you're on your own. Stay hydrated. There are claims by some studies that reduced hydration status might make it even more effective, but that feels just too risky. It's a short session, but it's not an easy day, so don't do it instead of recovery – though you won't need to be told that twice.)

That was the programme. Looking back at it, I'd say the training I put together wasn't perfect, but it wasn't terrible. I didn't see as much improvement as I'd have liked, but I saw as much as I probably deserved. I got all the gains you can get in eight weeks if you're not planning to train too much.

5

14,000 Calories a Day

'I think that my success is chiefly due to the good workings of my digestive organs. Once more was found true the saying of our manager Monsieur Manchon that "one wins a long road race by means of one's stomach",' said Francis Pelissier, after winning the 400-km Bordeaux–Paris race in 1922. In that race Pelissier told *Cycling* magazine that he ate mainly roast chicken, rice pudding and chocolate cake, with some cheese and bananas. He refrained from brandy or other spirits.

Sixty years later, there was a story about John Woodburn's Land's End to John O'Groats record in 1982 that has a nice echo of this. (You will remember Woodburn – he was the man who said, 'Any fool can get to Perth,' which is accepted as the wisest thing anyone has ever said about the End-to-End record.) The story has, in all honesty, proved a little difficult to pin down – Woodburn died a few years ago, the couple of his helpers on the ride that I checked it with were a bit unclear, and his biography makes no mention of it. The man who told me was a friend of Woodburn's, but wasn't involved in the ride. Here it is anyway.

His success in 1982 was his second ride. The previous year was the one where, exhausted and ill, he'd packed it in at Blair Atholl in the Cairngorms, made his comment about Perth, and gone home. On the earlier attempt his nutritional plan was based on the most relevant recent science, with a mainly liquid diet of glucose drinks, which in the end exacerbated the illness he'd been suffering from before he even started.

For the following year, he determined that he would do it differently. On the basis that on every other day of his life he ate three meals and generally that had worked quite well, he based his nutrition for the End-to-End on the same principle. The meals were normal food – fish and chips, pies – supplemented by traditional cycling foods, like malt loaf or fig rolls. The man who told me the story witnessed him somewhere north of Bristol barking, 'Chocolate cake!' at his helpers, who had to go and find some. There was a notorious incident where his team barged into a chip shop on a Friday evening, demanding instant service so they could catch up with him and feed him. (Though this story probably came from the year before – the reports are, alas, a bit unclear. Perhaps it was where the whole idea came from.)

The climax of the tale is, of course, that he broke the record second time out, with none of the distress of the previous year. It's an appealing story because it's one in the eye for science, one up for homespun wisdom, and a certain sort of cyclist likes just that sort of thing.

The science that ended up on the losing side wasn't anything much more complicated than dilute glucose syrup, simply because it delivers sugar very quickly. It would be liveable with for a short distance event (maybe even a 24-hour) but gets hard to stomach much beyond that, at least without a lot of habituation. There's also a good chance he was trying to consume too strong a mix. In the early days of liquid nutrition for sport, it was tempting to pile in the sugar and the energy because it was easy to swallow, and up till then, it was the swallowing that had been the bottleneck in the system. There was a glucose-fuelled period in the 1980s when racing cyclists had sore stomachs and incredibly bad teeth.

*

Nutrition is a very large part of the game if you're going long. Once you get over some basic humps of fitness and durability, it's almost the whole game. Or at least it feels like it when you're vomiting over your handlebars, while simultaneously feeling all the energy fading from your body and knowing that the only way to fix things is to do the one thing you can't do, which is eat.

In an ultra race, unless you go very slowly indeed, you cannot eat fast enough to replace the energy you are burning. A decent 24-hour racer will burn maybe 13,000–14,000 kcal during the race – it depends on their size, weight, aerodynamics and the course they're racing on. It also depends on how efficient their aerobic metabolism is. Different athletes riding with identical power outputs will still burn varying amounts of energy per mile.

I burned around 14,000 kcal on my first 24, a little less on my second, and there are some studies that show similar levels of expenditure for other riders. (I'm estimating my energy burn from my power data. This involves a bit of an assumption about my efficiency, since I'm taking a measure of output at the pedal rather than a measure of the energy actually expended.) Eating 580 kcal per hour to replace that, while riding at a reasonable effort level, would be very difficult indeed, unless you made up a fair proportion of it in fat, but fat isn't really your first priority.

In longer events the daily turnover drops, but not by all that much. There is also, it has to be said, a very large variation in the estimates from different studies. Between 9,000 and 17,000 kcals per day have been reported. Some of this variation will be measurement (it's generally being done by more sophisticated methods than power measurement), but a good bit of it will be genuine differences from rider to rider.

Nutrition can go wrong in many ways, almost all unpleasant. A friend who rode the 24-hour Championships in 2022, a year before my first go, told me, 'I had a pretty strong start. I hung onto about 22 mph clear through till about 4 a.m. But then I spent about an hour and a half in the woods, and never really got back on track.' I took the phrase 'in the woods' to be quaintly metaphorical. It was not. His nutrition had taken a dramatic southward turn, and his time in the woods was quite literal. He was behind a tree in a thicket a few yards from the A49.

The challenge is a reasonably simple one. You have, as previously mentioned, two main fuel sources for exercise:

fat and carbohydrate. There is a smaller role for protein, which is responsible for about 5% of your at-rest energy needs, but ideally you want to minimize the use of protein for energy because protein has more important roles, like constituting most of your legs.

The whole human metabolism in this area has evolved to frustrate the endurance athlete. There are vast reserves of energy stored in your body as fat – even the skinniest male athlete probably has 65,000 kcal worth, or 1,400 miles/23,000 km worth. Like a nuclear submarine, your energy supply should be well in excess of your durability. But of course, that doesn't work, because you burn a mix of fat and carbohydrate, and the proportions become more carb heavy as the intensity increases.

At rest, maybe 90% of the energy you need comes from fat. As the intensity increases, more and more carbohydrate is used, simply because your body can make the ATP molecules that prompt muscle contraction twice as fast from carbohydrate as it can from fat, and, as a bonus, you get more ATP per unit of oxygen via the carbohydrate reactions, so it's not only a quicker way to make ATP, it's also more efficient. By the time you get to around LT1 – the first lactate turn point – only about 50% of the energy is coming from fat. This is interesting, especially for something like a 24-hour race or an End-to-End, because LT1 is only just above the effort level you're aiming for. It's your never-exceed effort level. And if only 50% of the energy at that point is from fat, it means you've got more or less 50% to find from carbohydrate.

Of course, the 50% estimate is very rough. It varies by individual, by diet, by training. It also varies by how long the exercise has lasted. The fat ratio goes up over time, which might be one of the reasons that a drop in pulse at eight hours is such a regular feature of ultra rides – it could be a turning point in the role fat plays in fuelling. But at the moment we don't really know.

Be that as it may, you can't ride on fat alone. That didn't stop a friend of mine suggesting I should try it. When I told him I was taking up 24-hour riding, he said, 'I suppose you don't eat anything at all, you just rely on fat.' I can see the logic – it's a slow race. Well, you could try, but if your normal target pace demands something around 50% carbohydrate, you'd be very, very slow indeed. You'd have another problem, which is that your brain's preferred fuel source is carbohydrate. Your brain has no carbohydrate stores, so its supply of carbohydrate comes from your blood. If your blood sugar drops and you aren't replacing it, you will very quickly run into cognitive issues. Your capacity to make rational decisions will start to unravel, your motivation will decline. And as you know, you can't simply separate your brain from your physiology. Beyond that, you run into potentially more serious problems like simply blacking out.

There is a sort of backup system here. When your body reaches a certain level of carbohydrate starvation over a long period, your liver starts to use fatty acids to produce ketones. Ketones are a molecule that can be used as a kind of carbohydrate substitute by most of the organs and muscles, and especially by the brain. They enter the same energy cycle and fulfil a similar role. Unsurprisingly, since ketones constitute a whole other energy source, there's been a lot of interest in whether they might be used in sport. By the time your body starts making ketones of its own, you'd be in a pretty bad way from a performance point of view, but you can also introduce them via a ketone drink. These appeared around 2012 – they were used by some Olympic teams for the London Games, which was a bit of a gamble with something so new and untested. (It tells you something about the ever-present desperation for something new that might make that critical difference.)

Ever since there has been speculation about them, much of it quite wild. At one extreme I've heard claims of a 25% performance improvement. There have been calls for ketone drinks to be banned altogether. At the other end, there are plenty of athletes and sports scientists who are adamant they don't work at all.

The science is still rather uncertain. Most of the interest has focused on shorter distance events, like World Tour races and time trials, because that's where the money is. There seems to be an increasing consensus that over this sort of time span the difference to performance you might get from ketone drinks is pretty small. But there's also the much less investigated question of what might happen over longer distances. There is a clear possibility that ketones might work much better in more extreme nutritional states, especially as a readily available fuel for the brain and central nervous system. But, right now, it's not very clear. In any event, even if ketones have a beneficial effect, they won't replace the need for carbohydrate. There's no way round the physics of the required energy intake.

The other thing I would say from my encounters with ketones is that the taste might be a barrier. Nail-polish flavoured drinks are a hard thing to deal with at the best of times, and I don't think I'd thank you for one 15 hours into a race.

(My own experiences were that three post-ketone drink efforts produced two very good rides of around best-ever power over 20 minutes, and one very average ride. Hopeful though I was that maybe this was 'the one', I came to accept that the best I ever got was probably a placebo effect, one that didn't last all that long.)

So, to summarize, there is no getting around the need for carbohydrate. To put it simply, the more carbohydrate you can consume and absorb, the faster you'll go. The longer the event the more direct this relationship will get. It kicks in early – for a (mere) four- to six-hour road race, carbohydrate intake is a key factor in how strong a rider is in the later, critical stages. From the very start, riders will be hearing team directors on their radios reminding them to eat, eat, eat.

As the distance goes up, nutrition keeps increasing in importance. By 24 hours, the main predictor of performance is still aerobic ability and efficiency, but the availability of fuel is running in close second. Bear in mind that they're not independent – the greater your aerobic capacity, and the faster you can go, the more fuel you need per hour. If my sustainable LT1 effort is 280 watts and yours is 140 watts, I need double the fuel per hour. You'll be able to do your pace for much longer than I'll be able to do mine, unless I can keep fuel coming in and being absorbed faster than you. Unfortunately for me, the amount of carbohydrate you can store and the quality of your digestive system aren't linked to the size of your aerobic system. I could empty my fuel tank faster than you could empty yours, but I can't necessarily put it back any quicker. As time goes on, putting it back increasingly becomes the limiting factor.

Up the distance again, and the balance keeps shifting. By the time you get to a week-long event, and your wattage sinks to 100–150 watts but you're doing it for days and days, eating matters even more. It's one of the reasons that female athletes can perform so well in ultra races – they can eat as well as a male competitor.

Having said all that, there never really comes a point where food is the only question in town. You still need a degree of aerobic ability, because you need to keep the never-exceed LT1 lactate turn point at as high a power output as you can. That's simply because to maximize the proportion of fat you burn, your effort level needs to stay below LT1. If you were stupendous at eating but essentially a couch potato, your LT1 would be so low that any significant level of effort would shift you towards a more carbohydrate-intensive fuel mix, and your wondrous colon wouldn't be enough to compensate. As soon as you made any significant effort at all, you'd switch on all of your carbohydrate-burning systems and the amount of fat you'd utilize would drop.

The practical upshot of all this is simple. For ultra races, start with maximal carbohydrate stores, and keep them as full as possible for as long as you can. To do that, carbohydrate intake needs to be as much as you can manage. I might be able to beat you because my aerobic system is better. But Christoph Strasser can beat me by miles because, despite an aerobic system that maybe isn't all that different from mine, he can eat more.

Your priority problems are how much you eat, what you eat and where you get it. Your subsidiary problems are what you do when it all goes wrong – as it probably will. None of these are simple.

First things first, then. How much carbohydrate can a bike rider eat before they're in the woods? The traditional maximum as recently as the 2000s used to be 70 grams per hour, and was a pretty firm answer. Then things got more complicated. Different carbohydrates use different transport mechanisms to cross the gut membrane. For instance, maltodextrin and fructose use different mechanisms, and you can use them both at once. If you mixed maltodextrin and fructose in your drink, you could get to 90 g/hr – which is exactly what we used to do, adulterating ordinary energy drinks with fructose from the jam-making section of the supermarket. It was unbelievably sweet, and a little stressful on your digestion, but it worked perfectly well. It wasn't long before the manufacturers produced more palatable versions of the same idea.

There is other technology. The drinks I used for my 24-hours, made by a company called Maurten, were formulated as a sort of hybrid between a gel and a drink, which forms what Maurten calls a hydrogel in the stomach. The idea is that the structure of the hydrogel allows the carbohydrate to pass through the stomach more or less intact and move into the gut. The claim is that this reduces the stress on the stomach, meaning you can increase the amount of carbohydrate you consume. It's a claim that one nutritionist described to me as, 'Um, plausible, I suppose,' and another as, 'Look Michael, it's still just sugar.' On the other hand, the product has a very healthy following among pro athletes and teams, who frequently buy it in preference to a sponsor product.

These, and other innovations, mean that a lot of World Tour riders can consume carbohydrate at a rate of 120 g/hr, and some triathletes are rumoured to be managing even more, up around 160 g/hr. This is getting on towards double the traditional maximum from just a few years ago. In the last few seasons we've seen a lot of the old EPO-fuelled records for major climbs at the end of races being broken, and improved nutrition is one of the less cynical explanations. The riders just have more carbohydrate available. (There is, of course, no reason why you couldn't be doped to the eyebrows and simultaneously benefit from superior nutrition – in fact, the increased power output possible for a doped rider would increase their energy demand and mean that the two things would go together rather well. In some ways it would be the final bit of the jigsaw, the bigger fuel tank to go with the bigger engine.)

If you could consume 120 g/hr, that's around 450 kcal an hour, and for a 24-hour ride that would be just under 11,000 kcal. So you'd still be running in short, but not by very much. However, there is a major caveat to that 120 g/hr figure, which is that the World Tour riders are only attempting to do it for five or six hours. That's a very different show from all day and all night, or for a whole week. The longer you try to keep up a high carbohydrate intake, the more likely you are to run into problems. Realistically, you can't keep up that sort of consumption. The issue is what can you do?

For my first 24-hour, I consulted a chef. Alan Murchison is a friend, a very competent bike racer, the former owner of several Michelin-starred restaurants, and has had a very extensive career in more recent years cooking for cycling teams. He knows food, and he knows sport and he knows how to put them together. I figured that at a practical level he probably would, at the very least, be able to give me a good Plan A.

His reply to my first question ('Hi mate, can you help me with food for a 24-hour time trial?') arrived by WhatsApp and was characteristically blunt. 'The challenge here is to eat 80 g/hr of carb for 24 hours without shitting yourself.' The 80 grams was his suggestion of what was realistic as a starting point for an event that long. He was clear that how much an individual could deal with varied, and varied quite a lot. Some riders he'd worked with could deal with a lot more over that sort of period than others.

His suggestion was to mix solid food and energy drinks/gels. Plan A was to alternate hour and hour about, with odd-numbered hours of 80 g of carbohydrate in an energy drink, and even numbered hours of 40 g of carbohydrate in an energy drink and 40 g from food. He suggested traditional bike-racing foods. Things like rice cakes, a sort of solidified risotto, made in almost any flavour you might want to attempt. Or energy balls, which are simply oats, dates and peanut butter beaten to death in a food processor and rolled into balls.*

A rice cake or an energy ball would have 20 g of carbohydrate, so the idea was that in 'food' hours I drank the drink and had two solid items. This is another part of the challenge – you don't want to over- or under-eat. To maximize intake and minimize stress, you want to eat pretty close to (in my case) exactly 80 grams an hour. You spend a lot of your time adding these things up. 'I'm 25 minutes into my seventh hour, so I've had half of my 40 gram drink and half a rice cake, so that's 30 grams, so I'm... 4 grams behind schedule.' Some riders carefully keep the empty packets from energy foods so they can keep track – you can work from one pocket to another like a cricket umpire keeping track of an over with beads.

That's if it's all going well. A friend has a story about being sick over his handlebars, and then looking at the mess, trying to work out how much carbohydrate he now needed to catch up on. This is a disgusting story, but if you tell it to an ultra rider they nod in sympathy and understanding.

For my second 24-hour I made things a bit simpler from an arithmetic point of view by abandoning hours as my units. A 24-hour time trial works by riding repeated laps of various circuits, so instead I worked out how long each circuit would take, more or less, and then collected a circuit's worth of food and drink every lap, or every other lap depending on the length of the circuit in question. Then

---

* Alan has written several sporting cookbooks – I recommend them highly.

all I had to do was make sure I'd eaten and drunk it by the time I was due to collect more. So if a circuit was 80 minutes long, I simply picked up 110 grams of carbohydrate and consumed it by the next pick up, rather than try to keep track of 80 grams per hour as it went in and out of phase with seeing my crew. ('OK, so that's one bottle and a third of the next one, throw the two thirds away, collect a full one, drink half of that and eat two rice cakes, then have another rice cake and half an energy ball, throw the other half away… Hang on, I've got half a bottle of energy drink left. What am I supposed to do with that?') You can judge how brainless long rides make me from how much less stressful this trivial change made the whole process.

There's an irony here, which is that one of the ways I keep myself entertained on long rides is with maths, mainly converting my average speed into increasingly unlikely units. I once got as far as furlongs-per-fortnight (my first 24-hour averaged around 54,000 f/f, since you ask). So you might imagine the calorie calculations would appeal – but eating is just too important.

The other thing that Alan suggested was what's known as a fibre flush. At any given point, assuming you have a healthy diet, your gut contains maybe as much as a couple of kilos of fibre and associated water. If you follow a very low-fibre diet for a few days before the race, you can flush this out and not replace it. This has two attractions. First, it makes you a couple of kilos lighter, and that's not a disaster from a performance point of view. Second, it reduces the likelihood of needing a loo stop, of either a 'normal' or a 'very horrible emergency' variety, and this too is not a disaster. It also, at least anecdotally, somehow eases the process of ramming vast amounts of carbohydrate through your gut.

Alan's warning was that you could plan for around the first 12 hours. After that, anything might happen.

And he was right. In my first 24-hour, the first six hours were fine, the next six were a bit difficult. (This was, incidentally, my experience from 12-hour riding – but of course, in a 12-hour, that's enough.) At 12 hours in, around 2 a.m. on a very wet, very miserable night, I suddenly couldn't face anything at all. I couldn't tolerate drinks, gels, rice cakes, energy balls or any of the regular things in the plan. It wasn't that I was sick, or had stomach cramps, or anything else – I just couldn't put anything in my mouth without a horrible nausea.

I did about 90 minutes on nothing at all, while the crew shouted at me to take bottles and drink them. Mike in particular got quite cross about bottles being thrown back untouched. He's a teacher by profession, but even if I hadn't known that I'd have been able to guess. He would run alongside me at hand ups and deliver quite long lectures about what happens to long distance bike racers who don't eat enough.

What made the experience harder was that I couldn't come up with anything I actually did want. The team had a lot of options – energy chews, sweets, brioche buns, little pancakes, bananas, different drinks, various gels. And they were parked up not very far from an all-night gas station that was just packed with options, and a very surprised member of staff behind the night-window who had presumably been planning a quiet shift watching his iPad rather than six hours of fetching sweets for a crowd of bike riders who had appeared from nowhere. But I just couldn't think of anything I'd want to eat. In truth I couldn't really imagine ever eating again.

After the hiatus, I survived mainly on gels. There was a cyclical misery to it. I'd spend 20 minutes bracing myself for a gel. Then I'd squirt it into my mouth and hold it there for a while, summoning up the courage to swallow it. Then I'd swallow it. Then there would be about 90 seconds of awful nausea and a fight not to be sick. Then I'd start building up to the next one.

I've got two observations about this. The first is that holding the gel in my mouth probably had an ancillary benefit. There are numerous studies that show that even just rinsing your mouth with a sugary drink has benefits, apparently because it swindles your brain into thinking there's carbohydrate on the way. This is part of the whole central-governor area, where physiology and psychology overlap. You can get yourself through a tough spell, at least for a while, doing nothing but putting energy drink in your mouth for a few moments and spitting it out.

The second is that it was a kind of triumph. I kept eating, I kept going. I'd heard about how little fun eating can get to be in a long ride, but I'd never really appreciated what the reality might be like. I hated the gels. But I managed. I was falling short of my 80 g/hr target, but I was still hacking along at 40 g/hr, which was enough to keep riding.

For the next race a year later, I changed tack completely. I decided to see what might happen if I eliminated the solid foods, and just worked on energy drinks and a few supplementary gels. This was partly a suspicion that solids had been part of the problem – the simple act of chewing and swallowing became a struggle and I thought maybe that was where it had begun to come off the rails. The solids were also a hassle from the mathematical point of view of working out what I was consuming each hour. And since most of them were homemade, I liked the idea of not spending half the week preceding the race in the kitchen.

The liquid strategy wasn't a triumph either. At exactly the same point of the race, in the middle of a freezing cold night, I had the sudden sensation that someone had put a plug in the bottom of my stomach so that liquid wasn't emptying into my gut. My stomach felt like it was just filling up.

It produced a significant crisis. I was sick – very sick. I slowed dramatically. There was no real alternative to giving up – I couldn't see how I was coming back from this because I felt so dreadful. Not tired, but ill, like I was trying to ride a bike through 'flu, and was sapped of all energy. I'd been eating well up to that point, so this was clearly not literally true. But perhaps, like the reverse of the effect you get from just putting energy drink in your mouth, my brain already knew we were in trouble and was pulling down the blinds.

I rode back to the team and told them I was finished. I thanked them for their help. They said that was OK, and gave me an anti-sickness tablet, and suggested a little rest. Then Chris Murray, the previous year's 24-hour champion, gave me some jelly snake sweets. Only when she handed them to me did I realize they were the greatest food on Earth – I ate about six at once. Then she and Mike gently loaded me back on the bike, put the rest of the snakes in my pocket and pushed me off again into the dark. Within 10 or 15 minutes, I was fine. It was bizarre, as if I'd been switched off and on again. I ate all the snakes, then did the rest of the race on an almost exclusive diet of Haribo sweets, brioche buns and rice pudding, which was almost as far from that year's Plan A as it was possible to go.

Part of my inspiration for the doomed liquid 24-hour had come from a conversation with Christoph Strasser, whose multiple Race Across America victories have been achieved on a purely liquid diet. I perhaps missed the important bits. His drink of choice isn't even a sports drink – it's Ensure Plus, which is designed as a meal replacement for hospital patients, the very ill and the elderly.

In one of my favourite ultra rider interview moments, I asked him, 'Doesn't that get very, very boring after a week? Litres of the same drink?'

'No, it's fine,' he said. 'It comes in chocolate and vanilla. You can have a good meal or a good performance.'

The other thing about Strasser's RAAM approach is that he switched to purely liquid three days before the race. 'I got hungry for the first day or two,' he said. 'And then I was fine, for as long as I needed to ride. You don't feel full, and even after eight days I don't feel at all sick.'

The question of boredom doesn't really do the potential problems of a limited diet justice. The reason I took so many seemingly random food options to races was because of another mortal enemy of the long distance snacker:

flavour fatigue. My most vivid memory of my last 12-hour Championships was the final bottle of electrolyte drink handed up at 11 hours. It was the same as every other bottle – a mild lemony flavour. Except that last one tasted like it was full of seawater. Suddenly all I could taste was the half-a-gram (or whatever it was) of salt. The orange-flavoured non-electrolyte drink I tried instead tasted just plain weird – it was like nothing I'd ever tried to drink before. The only thing that didn't taste odd was a bottle of flat Coke that I snatched from someone else's support team. But it was almost equally strange in a whole other way. It tasted amazing. I knew it was just regular Coke. But I also knew it was the greatest thing I'd ever drunk, and that if I could formulate and market something that under normal circumstances tasted like that to everyone else, I'd eventually have all the money in the world and people would still be looking for more to give me.

Partly it's the sheer repetition, and partly it's the effects on your body of the extreme efforts, but after a while the flavours of things go funny. It's a real issue when most of the regular energy products you get used to in cycling are sweet – if you suddenly can't cope with sweet flavours, you're in real trouble. In Race Across America, Shu Pillinger took to cucumber smoothies in the quest for something that wasn't sweet. Most of the rice cakes I used in the early part of my first 24-hour were smoked ham and cheese flavoured, not because I liked them, but because they weren't sweet. Little finger sandwiches are another option, or even something like sausage, which provides almost no carbohydrate at all, but is just a counter-flavour. It's one of the reasons that John Woodburn's 'three meals a day' End-to-End might have worked, because it had savoury to balance the sweet.

Similarly, over a Danish pastry in a Cambridge café, UK-based ultra runner Mark Turner told me that for things like the Spine Race (a week-long, midwinter run along the 268-mile Pennine Way, stretching from Derbyshire in England into the Scottish Borders) he worked on a mix of energy products and a substantial amount of what he described as just 'normal food' – even things that seem improbable to someone like me, such as Peperami and beef jerky, even some chips or a Magnum ice cream when he could get them. 'But the problem was repetition. On my first Spine Race, all the food bags I'd sent to the aid stations had the same foods in them. By the third or fourth stop, instead of just transferring the food to my backpack, I had to try to trade a lot of it for other things with other runners who were in the same position. You never really know what you're going to want until you get there.'

Turner's approach focuses on calories from a broader range of sources, rather than just on carbohydrate. For his Bob Graham Round (a run that climbs 42 peaks in the Lake district in 24 hours), he found one of the major problems was eating while running at any sort of intensity. 'I tried things like pork pies,' he said. 'And you chew and chew and chew, then you add some drink to see if that helps... it's like a washing machine. In the end one of the things I did for that race was make little bags of mashed potato with a little butter, and I could squeeze it out of the bag like an energy gel.'

14,000 CALORIES A DAY

You can train to eat. When Strasser attacked the 24-hour record, he trained the nutrition side of the equation for six months on the run in, in an attempt to adapt to 120 g/hr, a World Tour rider's target, but pushing it out to the full length of a 24-hour ride. It's simple in concept: you start your ride with a full-ish stomach (just have a good breakfast and head out), then consume carbohydrate during the ride, aiming to build up to something around 120 g/hr. Some people can manage more, at least for moderate length rides or races.

The principle is the same as any other training: you push past what's completely comfortable and hopefully you adapt. Jon Baker, a sports scientist working with World Tour riders, told me, 'Most recreational cyclists can cope with maybe 60 grams an hour, for a few hours. Then they stop wanting to eat anything at all. The pros can often do 100 to 120 grams an hour, and they can do it for a full race. It's training that lets them do this. You just push it and see what happens – how do you tolerate it? To be blunt about it, are you farting a lot? Is there a really unpleasant gassy feeling? That's how you find your limits.'

You could even try doing it without the cycling; there's no fundamental reason why you can't get at least some of the benefits from stressing your system with energy products and carbohydrate-rich foods while sitting on the sofa and watching old episodes of *Friends*. But it has to be said that it does work better as part of a ride. You'll put on less weight for a start (a four-hour ride on the sofa with 120 g of carbohydrate an hour is getting on towards 1,900 kcal). And by doing it while exercising you will also be training your gut to manage that kind of load with a reduced blood supply.

The other issue you might train, or at least gain some experience with, is the issue of digestion and body position. You're designed to digest stuff in a more or less upright position. You're certainly not designed to do it in a prone(ish) aerodynamic bike-riding position. You rapidly learn that if it's not downhill from your mouth to your stomach when you're in position, you're going to have to sit up to eat or drink. For multi-day rides it produces other considerations. Quite a few long distance racers and record riders have resorted to jumping up and down in a layby or a car park in an attempt to, as one of them put it, 'Get things to move downwards a bit.'

There are other problems you'll run into on longer races, but they can be hard to train for. Over the course of several days, even if your gut will tolerate it, eating 10,000 kcal a day (or whatever your target is) gets hard. You get oesophageal swelling, so just the basic act of swallowing becomes difficult. Your mouth can get horribly tender – even after one of my 24-hour races, when I tried to eat a post-race steak and some chips at the hotel the food was almost unbearably painful against the roof of my mouth. I had to eat in tiny little mouthfuls. Clearly, just a day or two into a long race, the chances are I'd be far past the point where I could even contemplate something like a nice crisp baguette.

In RAAM, Shu Pillinger told me that as the exhaustion started to bite, she began to get mouth ulcers and, on top of that, sunburned lips. She just couldn't eat as much as she needed to, it was too painful. It meant a change of plan, to foods and liquids she could tolerate.

That sort of problem and improvised solution is one of the reasons most serious support crews include a nutritionist. On Pillinger's RAAM, she was supported by the human performance lab of pharmaceutical company GSK, which meant she started out with an analysis of what exactly her nutritional demands were. She had, for example, a sports drink that was formulated to balance her required salt intake with her planned carbohydrate intake.

On the race, the team nutritionist prepared all the food and loaded it onto the bike at stops. Then over the radio they'd read the menu for the section. 'They'd just say, on the left of the box [on the top tube of the bike] you've got some avocado wraps, on the right you've got some biscuits and peanuts, and they'd tell me what I needed to eat and when. They'd have worked out what I needed, and figured out how to give it to me, and give it to me in a way that worked at that part of the race – most of the time I need carbohydrates, but I wanted them to come as savoury flavours. Every time I stopped I peed into a bottle, so they could check my hydration. I think the only time that got a bit low they just said I wasn't getting back on the bike till I'd drunk an extra bottle. It worked really well.'

Long, unsupported ultra races bring in a different consideration, which is where, practically speaking, your calories and drinks are going to come from. You can carry perhaps as much as the first day with you. After that, you're going to have to buy them as you go. It's one of the few sports where mid-race shopping is a key part of the race.

You're not likely to find a big selection of sport-specific products in a gas station, or even in very many supermarkets. Christoph Strasser said that he was 'pretty frightened' at the start of his first Transcontinental Race, just because he was off the very controlled sort of food planning that he was used to, and which he credited with a lot of his success in supported events. 'I wasn't sure what I'd be able to get, how it would work. But I was really surprised. When I had to survive for four days mainly on Snickers and Coke, it was kind of OK. I could not have imagined that working, but it did.'

I had an almost inverse conversation with Fiona Kolbinger. I asked her why she was so good at unsupported ultra events. There are clearly a lot of reasons, but among the ones she lit on first was, 'I can eat crap for days on end.' In the first two days of her winning TCR ride she said, 'I think I ate about 50 Snickers bars, and not a lot else. You can lose a long distance race by not being fit enough. But you win a long distance race in the stomach, and I'm lucky. Mine is pretty resilient. I race on whatever I can get from a supermarket – it's all normal stuff, nothing special. And I do all my riding and training on junk as well. You can't eat to cover all the energy you use in a race. Even if you're a light rider, you're burning 10,000 to 15,000 kcal a day. But I think that if you can maybe cover 80% of that, you're sort of on a level.'

Among the riders I talked to, there wasn't a huge consensus on what you grab from a supermarket. On Pillinger's TCR ride (she's ridden both RAAM and TCR), she said the biggest score was the day she found some cold roast potatoes. 'That was such a supermarket find. They were amazing.' Other riders look for bread, pastries, sweets, but also things like roast chicken, even some salad bits, despite the lack of energy density. ('Cherry tomatoes,' said Emily Chappell, 'I'll grab some of those and put them in my bar bag – they are just delicious.') On the really long rides there start to be things other than just carbohydrate to consider. You need to think at least a bit about the vitamins and minerals you'd need in normal life. And above all, you need to keep eating. What you eat is almost secondary to the absolute requirement that you keep doing it.

Most of the headlines around long distance nutrition are about carbohydrate and other nutrients. But you also need to drink. Long races, especially if they last for days in hot conditions, mean hydration matters – you don't have to be all that dehydrated before performance starts to slip. Although, it interests me that it's not actually something that came up all that often in conversations with riders or sports scientists as a source of major concern.

Jon Baker's take on it was fairly typical – his suggestion was that in most circumstances in a long event, you can drink to thirst. 'It's an evolutionary response,' he said. 'There is a reason it works. Also, if you need to pee more often than you would in normal life, you're probably drinking too much. If you're peeing a lot less, well, then you need to drink a bit more.' An alternative approach for supported riders is to check their body weight at stops, and make sure it's staying reasonably stable, or to do what Pillinger did and check their urine. But as long as it's something you're paying attention to, under most circumstances, your hydration is probably all right. Almost everyone has multiple bottles of liquid on their bike, so unless you run out it's easy to keep on top of it.

In some ways the sheer duration of ultra events makes it less critical than it might be in something like a marathon. You're not working at anything like the same intensity, or sweating as hard. You've got more time to adapt. And you're not operating as close to the edge. Elite marathon runners often aim to finish at least a little dehydrated, because the reduction in weight counts for more than the reduction in performance. But it only works if it's carefully managed – they're aiming for a pretty small window. No one is trying to do this sort of thing in an ultra race.

One of the reasons you use quite coarse-seeming measures like thirst and urination is that sweat rate varies from person to person. It's very hard to generalize. You can, of course, monitor it more closely – there are several sweat monitoring devices on the market that can give you a better guide to how much you're losing. If I was riding a long race in hot conditions, at the very least I'd want to pick up a general picture of sweat rates from training. But it's not something I ever did for the 24-hour races.

The associated issue is sodium losses in sweat. Again, this is more critical in 'ordinary' long events, like marathons or Ironman. The rate of sodium loss varies even more from individual to individual than sweat rate. Quoted rates range from 200 mg to 2,500 mg per litre. In an ultra, you're probably covered by what you're going to do naturally. It helps that ultra riders almost always use solid food as well as just drinks, and most of that will have some sodium in it.

Some riders take salt tablets, sometimes because they've had their sweat and sodium loss rates measured and know that there's an issue they need to be on top of, but more often as a sort of general insurance policy – 0.5–1 g/hr would be an adequate safeguard in shortish ultra events in warm environments. Since your sweat will always be more dilute than your blood, as you sweat your blood sodium levels won't really drop that much. The bigger risk is over-hydration. This is hyponatremia, where excessive fluid lowers your blood sodium concentration, leading to symptoms that start out with headache, confusion and poor balance and move on into seizures and even death – there have been several deaths in marathons in the last few years from hyponatremia, usually among slower runners whose sweat rates are quite low but who are convinced they need to keep drinking as much as they can. That's why you shouldn't attempt to drink significantly more water than you're sweating.

In my races, while I've never got close to the danger zone, my problem has been more one of over-hydration than under-, which was just a result of my reliance on a steady supply of carbohydrate drinks and the occasional bottle of tea in the middle of the night. In the last couple of events I've done I've had to pee more often than is entirely convenient. My next iteration of long distance nutrition will be less reliant on drinks for just that reason, unless it's very hot. It is, like everything else about how much you eat, what you eat, where it comes from and what you do or don't wash it down with, irritatingly personal. You find out by trial and error. But mainly error.

6

Reinventing the Bike Race and the Rise of the Amateurs

The most obvious characteristic of an ultra race is its length. My initial assumption that an ultra was probably just a long version of a short race proved to be gloriously wide of the mark – length affects everything. But there are other differences as well, which change how the races work and how you have to approach them. Ultra races aren't quite part of the same ecosystem as shorter races. They haven't developed through the same routes, or been underpinned by sponsorship and professional riders. And that means their basic culture is not the same – not only is an ultra race not just a long version of a short race, it's fair to say that a lot of the people riding them are a little bit different as well.

Early road races like the Tour de France may have begun as something that feels close to a modern ultra race, but they didn't stay that way. By the middle of the twentieth century, pro events had very largely turned into something you'd recognize as modern UCI-style racing. There were teams, there was a peloton, there were breakaways, there were tactics. There were team cars, drugs, reporters, fans by the roadside. Distances came down, and the speeds went up, so the races stopped lasting two nights and a day and started to be something that began in mid-morning and finished in time for the next day's papers.

There were a few exceptions. Bordeaux–Paris ran until the 1980s, as a 360-mile (560-km) event beginning at around 3 a.m., and finishing late the following afternoon. To add to the oddness, riders did the first four to five hours in a group, then they stopped for breakfast (yes, really) at around 7 a.m. Then they met up with a group of pacing motorbikes, traditional Dernys – the sort of buzzing super-moped you still sometimes see leading out a track Keirin. The rest of the race was done in rider/Derny pairs. Physically it was very demanding. There's really no such thing as a peloton in that sort of event because there's no advantage to you and your pacer in sitting behind someone else and their pacer. In practical terms it's close to a solo effort, rather like a Tour stage of old. Pro riders didn't like it very much, and it became a novelty race before eventually it faded away altogether. The last edition was 1988. It's still mourned by a certain sort of traditionalist like myself, despite the fact that most of us are too young to remember it, and would under no circumstances have been prepared to do it.

It's tempting, then, to conclude that long distance, solo racing essentially died, and then resurrected itself in the twenty-first century. This is at best half true. The long distance riders never really went away, they were just doing other things. For most of the twentieth century, especially in the UK, touring was the biggest part of cycling. At one end, that covered a club run noodling around the countryside for a few hours. But at the other, it included some demanding riding. A friend of mine recalls a solo youth hostelling trip round the North of Scotland, taken when he was a student in the 1970s, and which lasted a fortnight covering anything up to 200 miles a day. He stayed in hostels and bothies, found his own supplies, and made it all the way to Cape Wrath at the north-western tip of Great Britain – and not by the ferry across the Kyle of Durness that lets you ride to the cape over a few miles of rutted track. Instead, he rode for miles up the western coastline on a mix of rough tracks and bits of straightforward wilderness where there wasn't even that. He met other riders on his way who were doing something similar.

The randonneurs had similar appetites but a more regimented style. Randonnée events cover big mileages, on set routes, but aren't a race. The most famous of them is Paris–Brest–Paris, which started life in 1891 as a very long pro road race, before it gradually morphed into what it is now – a 750-mile (1,200-km) randonnée that runs every four years with a field limited to 8,000. And despite the fact you need to qualify by doing official shorter rides of up to 375 miles, it fills up every time. While it's no longer a race, it still has a time limit of (for most riders) 90 hours, or nearly four days. That's an average of eight-and-a-bit miles per hour, but as you'll have come to expect, the clock keeps running when you're asleep, so you wouldn't want to get it confused with a soft event. It's done with limited support, so it's into sleeping under hedges territory for many. There's no 'winner' but the first finisher is usually home in 42–43 hours.

The UK has the even longer, but rather younger London–Edinburgh–London, which started in 1989, is about 950 miles and, again, is non-competitive. The time limit is 128 hours – a bit over five days. There are other shorter events running in the UK on the same basis, traditionally focused on 200, 400 and 600 km, with both a minimum and a maximum time limit so you can't make it a race even if you want to. Randonnées are a whole subculture of cycling, and perhaps its least flashy. The discipline is about quiet self-sufficiency and reliability, ideals that hark back to the earliest days of cycling. The fact that it's not quite a race but not quite *not* a race means the riders need to have a certain level of both commitment and ability, but makes the event an experience that's more communal than competitive. The objective is not to win, but to succeed, and while only one person can win, lots of people can succeed.

All the same, the mid-twentieth century was not a competition-free zone as far as long rides were concerned. In the UK, for example, the place-to-place record breaking continued. Having ridden the Tour de France in 1928 and 1931, and winning Paris–Brest–Paris in 1931, the Australian professional Hubert Opperman came to the UK in 1934 and in possibly the most productive fortnight in record-breaking history broke five records, including the End-to-End in 57 hours, and the 1,000 miles in 74 hours.

Opperman was a superlatively good rider. If he'd come from anywhere nearer the European centre of the cycling world in the 1920s and 1930s than Australia, he might well be a household name to this day. In 1928, he won the Bol d'Or 24-hour track race despite a saboteur filing through the chains of both his race and spare bikes. He borrowed his interpreter's street bike, with mudguards and upright handlebars, and won anyway. That was the sort of rider he was.

Place-to-place records in that era were very much a UK phenomenon, but Opperman also broke the Australian transcontinental record from Fremantle to Sydney, covering 2,875 miles in 13 days – something that feels very much of a piece with modern ultra racing. A modern TCR racer will have sympathy for the miles of soft sand dunes he sometimes had to carry his bike across. He even made the discovery, long before everyone else, that sleeping for 10–15 minutes at a time could sustain him for days on end. (He later became a politician, and served as a cabinet minister between 1960 and 1966 in the Australian Liberal governments of Sir Robert Menzies and Harold Holt. His whole life was conducted at an irritating level of over-achievement.)

Place-to-place records were a vital refuge for women especially. In an era when women's racing was very limited and women's professional racing was simply non-existent, the history of place-to-place riding as a means of selling stuff meant that it was much too late to keep out what the magazines sniffily referred to as 'cash riders'.

Marguerite Wilson was only 19 when she turned pro for the Hercules cycle company in 1937. In 1939, she set one of the great Land's End to John O'Groats records, of just under 71 hours. Her End-to-End ran from 29 August to 1 September, meaning that Prime Minister Neville

Chamberlain made his broadcast announcing the outbreak of war as she was approaching John O'Groats. All the same she continued for a further 13 hours to complete the 1,000-mile record as well – this she broke by a shattering 31 hours. This was despite riding through a nation preparing for war, to the extent that when she looked ahead for the lights of Wick, where her 1,000 miles would finish, they had already been blacked out.

She managed to continue riding and record breaking through the early years of the war, and by 1941 she held every UK record that was available to her. *The Golden Book of Cycling* (a slightly strange, single-copy, hand-calligraphed book that looks like it was created by a monk in the fourteenth century, and is the hall of fame for twentieth-century cycling in the UK) described her as 'The greatest girl rider in cycling history'.

She was followed by an even greater 'girl rider'. The peerless Eileen Sheridan was 4 feet 11 inches of pure athlete. She started racing in 1945, and by 1950 had made the amateur racing scene in the UK entirely her own – especially the longer distances. Her 12-hour riding was on a par with the best men of the era. In 1951, having run out of amateur races to dominate, she turned pro to chase records, also for Hercules. Like Wilson before her, she broke every record there was, and usually by even bigger margins. At the time of writing, in 2024, four of her records still stand, more than 70 years after she set them. (They are: London–Edinburgh, London–Liverpool, London–Bath–London, and London–Portsmouth–London.) Despite being the most sought-after of all the records, her Land's End to John O'Groats record stood for 36 years, and her 1,000-mile record lasted until it was broken by Lynne Taylor in 2002.

The 1954 End-to-End moved the event into a different era. Eileen Sheridan rode the 870-odd miles of the pre-Forth Road Bridge route in 59 hours 11 minutes. It was seven hours faster than the previous year's amateur record of Edith Atkins and fully 11 hours faster than the old pro record of Marguerite Wilson. She took two hours off her bike at John O'Groats to eat a fried breakfast, then, like Wilson, got back on board to break the 1,000-mile record by over 10 hours. ('What's another 130 miles?' she shrugged. She was not like the rest of us.) Her 1,000-mile record was only a couple of hours slower than the then men's mark.

For all Sheridan's upbeat approach, the ride that took the End-to-End and the 1,000-mile records was as Herculean as her sponsor would have wished. The weather was largely against her, with long periods of rain and headwind. She had hallucinations of mermaids, polar bears, ghosts, groups of people standing on the road pointing her the wrong way. For miles she was convinced that an inexplicable giant wooden platform on wheels was following her. When she stopped, which was not very often, she had to be fed by her helpers because her hands were so blistered from the bars that she couldn't feed herself. In the last hours, supporters sang to her and ran alongside offering her flowers picked from the verges to keep her going. Her manager, Frank Southall, a hardman record breaker himself and a rival of Hubert Opperman's from before the war, was repeatedly reduced to tears by the extremes Sheridan was prepared to push herself to.

She retired shortly after that ride. She used her salary and bonuses to buy a house in Isleworth in West London, where she lived until she died in 2023 at the age of 99. She remained very active in cycling her whole life, but never again rode competitively. She did, however, find time to become British national 500-metre K2 canoeing champion in 1956. She remains to this day the ultimate hero to most of the long distance record aspirants in the UK.

While it didn't always have the raw excitement of the early days when bicycles themselves were an innovation and the distant horizon was an invitation, this side of the sport trundled on. Later riders – Pauline Strong, Lynne Taylor, John Woodburn, Gethin Butler – continued in a discipline that was almost unchanged since it was invented. The 12- and 24-hour races in the UK continued as well, again with their roots and bureaucracy firmly in the Victorian era. As the twentieth century wore on, it all got less and less fashionable. By the time I started my first 12-hour in 2000, it felt like what we were doing was at least 10% historical reenactment.

Elsewhere, things began to change. Cycling in the US went in a different direction as early as the 1970s. Most of Europe was still hanging on to cycling as a very traditional, working-class sport that still had strong ties to cycling as transport – the dramatic decline in the sport's popularity in the 1960s and 1970s in Europe and (especially) the UK was tied to a perception of it as something for the old-fashioned and the poor. If you were riding a bike, it was because you couldn't afford a car.

In the US, they got out the far side of that a bit sooner. By the early 1970s, the US experienced a bike boom, as cycling transitioned to an aspirational leisure activity that had nothing much to do with transport. For many riders there was a child-like fun to cycling. Mountain biking had its roots in California's legendary 'Repack' races in the mid-1970s – where riders hurled themselves down an old, precipitous, twisty dirt road in Marin County on home-modified cruiser bikes. They called it 'Repack' because the grease in an old coaster hub brake would burn away entirely and need to be repacked after just a couple of overheated rides. The prizes for the deeply informal races were mainly smokable, the crashes were legendary, and if you look down a list of the riders you find quite a few names that later became much better known for the sort of bike brands that could not have been further away in their ethos from the staid, classical frame builders of Europe – Gary Fisher, for example, or the brand Marin, named for the county, or Specialized, started by Repacker Mike Sinyard.

Mountain biking was a vital cog in the changing perception of cycling as a sport. People took up mountain biking who'd never have taken up road cycling, and who then found their way to the road anyway because it was a more efficient way to train, and normally easier to do from your front door. Because they hadn't arrived via a traditional route, they had no connections with traditional road racing, or even much knowledge of it – the US was a very long way from the pro road racing heartlands of Western Europe. As if it was the early days of the bicycle all over again, they started inventing from the beginning, and perhaps unsurprisingly one of the directions they went in was endurance. The 'Century Ride' of 100 miles became a staple challenge, and it eventually got imported back across the Atlantic and formed the nucleus of the sportive boom of the late 2000s, also for a cohort of riders who were not from traditional cycling.

There was an anarchic nature to this. Informal challenges started to grow – ride to all four corners of a state. Ride the perimeter of a state. Ride from coast to coast. Ride from one end of a state to the other. The records were kept among friends and acquaintances, the rules were negligible. It was a member of this community, John Marino, who challenged three other riders to a race across America, from Santa Monica in California to the Empire State Building in New York City in 1982. He called it the Great American Bicycle Race, but it quickly became simply the Race Across America. The fact that just about the oldest ultra race is still probably the most famous makes the whole thing feel like instant history. The first race was won by Lon Haldeman, in just under 10 days at an average speed of 12.5 mph. He won the following race as well, and returned in 1992 to win the tandem category.

ABC's *Wide World of Sports* covered the races for the first five editions, which generated the sort of free publicity a modern race organizer with an Instagram account can only dream of. Despite the arduous nature of the race, its immensely picturesque premise was an immediate hit. In exactly the same way the early Tours de France grabbed the imagination, RAAM returned the sport to its most fundamental nature. The route has varied over the years – the start has always been in California or (just three times) Oregon, with finishes so far in New York, Georgia, Washington DC,

New Jersey, Florida or Maryland. The distance has always been close to 3,000 miles.

Similar supported races started to spring up, both in the US and in Europe, not least because the popularity of RAAM meant there was a need for a qualifying system based on other, generally shorter, races.

The major divergence between supported and unsupported had its roots in US anarchy as well. The Tour Divide started in 2008. It's a ride that covers the full length of the 2,700-mile Great Divide mountain bike trail, following the Rocky Mountains from Canada to Mexico. It is unsupported to such an extent that it barely exists as a formal entity. There's no entry process, no prizes, no sponsorship. GPS trackers are optional. Riders just turn up at either end of the trail on the appointed day (usually the second Friday in June to roughly coincide with the solstice) and set off. You don't even have to be that organized if it doesn't suit your schedule or your personality – Tour Divide rides done as a time trial at any time of the season are recognized. It's self-sufficient, and very tough. There are 60,000 metres of altitude gain, the towns are often far apart and sometimes not much to get excited about when you get there, there are some sections where riders have to push or carry their bikes, mechanical problems are frequent and difficult to cope with, bears are a danger in some areas and the rewards for success verge on nothing at all. It is, in many respects, an epitome of ultra riding. You do the Tour Divide for the love of it because there is no other conceivable reason.

It was a Tour Divide winner and record holder, the British rider Mike Hall, who took his experiences in the US and created the Transcontinental Race in Europe in 2013, as an unsupported crossing of a continent, this time mainly on surfaced roads. Its starts and finishes vary, as does its direction of travel across Europe, though it's usually a diagonal from top left to bottom right or the reverse. Unlike most of its predecessors, the TCR doesn't have a fixed route, just a start, a finish, a handful of obligatory checkpoints, and some compulsory sections (known as parcours) that you have to cover, normally on gravel or unmade roads to add to the difficulty. As with almost all ultra events, it's a time trial. You can't ride with anyone else for more than a few moments. Mike Hall was killed riding the similar 5,500-km Indian Pacific Wheel Race in Australia in 2017 when he was hit by a car driver near Canberra. His race has continued, run (and ridden) by his colleagues and friends.

TCR spawned numerous similar races, the majority of them a bit shorter. In this book I've tended to focus on the best-known races, the ones that attract the best riders and the most attention. There are others with brilliant extra challenges, different tactical requirements. The Pan-Celtic Race, for example, uses ferries to connect the nations that form its course, meaning that there are substantial gains to be made by catching the early ferry and sleeping aboard while you're still moving, and equivalent losses if you miss it. In my previous book *Faster*, about shorter more 'normal' races, it was obvious that the main focus had to be the Tour de France, the classics and the Olympics because in the end they're the ultimate aspiration of almost everyone involved. In ultra racing, it's not that straightforward. There are plenty of riders picking races simply because that particular route, country or event appeals, and plenty of riders entering even the biggest races with little interest in winning or any result beyond making it to the finish in time for the party that usually acts as the time limit.

Increasingly the unsupported races are taking over from the supported ones, because of their simplicity and their relative lack of expense. They also fit with an amateur ethos. There are a lot of riders who've come to feel that the idea of several hundred riders and teams doing something like crossing North America with a fleet of supporting RVs and vehicles and many, many flights to get people and equipment in position isn't quite what they ought to be doing. Many unsupported races, like TCR, have category recognition for riders who ride to the start and then back home from the finish, or get there and back without flying. For some events, entry is conditional on one or both of these. Part of the appeal of long distance cycling is precisely the lack of impact on the lands you cross. Maybe there isn't much point in crossing a continent like a leaf on the wind if you get to the start line on a Boeing 777.

Ultra racing can be low impact in other ways. When Fiona Kolbinger became the first woman to win TCR overall in 2019, it aroused a lot of general press interest that the race had never previously attracted. At the finish in Brest, a modest press pack descended and struggled to find much sign of the race. There's no finish gantry. There's not even really a line. Rory Kemper, from the organizers Lost Dot, told me, 'I explained to them that she'd arrive, I'd accompany her inside the hostel that was the finish HQ, I'd stamp her brevet card, take a photo or two, and that was it. That was the finish. We didn't want a huge scrum of photographers in there, because it's an exhausting race, it can be a bit emotional at the end. So she arrived, I brought her inside, we stamped her card with just the two of us and a few volunteers in there, and they took a few photos. Then she headed off to a hotel. One of the journalists, quite a big name in French sports writing, said to me that it was just so beautiful. It wasn't at all what he expected. But he realized there was something pure about the event. It wasn't about the finish, it was about the race, and he absolutely got it.'

That level of traditional press interest was a bit of an aberration. These races have a different media presence. If you want to spectate, you watch a dot creep across a map on a screen. If you want to know more, you follow the dot on social media. It's another expression of the idea that the event is the race, not the result. You almost stop being a fan looking at the race from the outside and start seeing the race from the inside through its participants. It can be strangely frustrating at times – a dot does something odd, and it's hours before you find out why, and when you do it's because a rider posts a cryptic photo that leaves you scrabbling around on Street View trying to work out what it means. But it's involving in a different way from watching the Tour de France on TV. In some ways it harks back to the early Tours and coverage that was just as episodic, as well as partial, erratic and occasionally made up in an attempt to make sense of results that were hard to explain and that stemmed from events with no witnesses.

One of the questions is what would happen if the professionals arrived? There's no doubt that among the current

World Tour pelotons you could find some riders who'd be very good at this sort of thing. They've all got the right sort of physiology, and winnowing down by digestive durability and psychological resilience would not get rid of them all. Lachlan Morton, of the EF Education–EasyPost team, has done several ultra rides, including the GBDURO in the UK, from Land's End to John O'Groats, a 30-day record lap of Australia, and his 'Alt Tour', an unsupported solo ride round the route of the 2021 Tour de France. All of these became social media events.

According to Rory Kemper from Lost Dot, 'We've talked about how someone like that might change TCR, especially after some of Lachlan's rides, because they got a lot of publicity for the team. It hasn't really happened, yet, but we're still not very sure how it would fit with the amateur ethos we've always had. A lot of the culture of the race isn't written down, it's just that people learn what the good and bad things to do are. Everyone should get to the finish line, be able to look each other in the eye and know they've all been through the same thing. There's an integrity to it, if something happens on the road you hope that people will self-report anything. It's hard not to worry that we'd lose something if the race became professionalized. At the moment if someone does something like take a prohibited road [some roads are off-limits because they're perceived as too dangerous], we normally accept that they weren't trying to get an advantage, they just made a mistake, and we give them a time penalty that's not intended to be a punishment, it's just to keep the race fair. That sort of thing would come under a lot of pressure.'

Pro riders from pro teams would come to a race expected to get results. The current system, which takes a lot on trust and assumes that everyone is basically honest, would find that hard to cope with. If a major team puts £100,000 behind a rider in salary, costs, other races missed and post-event recovery time, they might not be very sympathetic to a cuddly regulatory regime that takes as its first aim making sure everyone enjoys the race and gets to the finish. To protect its investment, a pro team would expect clearer rules and explicit penalties for breaking them, whether you meant it or not. It would demand doping tests equivalent to the ones its riders are already subject to, so random out-of-competition tests as well as tests during the race. These are not things that currently happen, and in the middle of a week-long non-stop race, the logistical challenges of dope testing might be interesting and expensive. (Do you flag someone down, and they just lose the time it takes to pee and go through the process of packing up the sample and filling in the forms, which could take between 15 minutes and a couple of hours? Do you stop the clock, and invite the cynical rider to take as long as possible to produce a sample and, I don't know, maybe have a 'free' sleep while they wait?)

The other thing a pro team would want is much more coverage. It would probably remain in a social media environment, but it would be hard to see how a single rider could produce and edit enough material and updates while also doing the actual race. It could end up as a strange duathlon of bike riding and video production. Would organizers end up having to allow an accompanying media reporter per rider? That's how they've solved a similar problem in the world of long distance offshore yacht racing. But it would profoundly alter the experience of doing the race if you've got someone on a moto with you the whole way, even if they're not allowed to help.

It would also mean that the sport would really need a recognized governing body. At the moment there isn't really one. A lot of the races run under their own rules, others run under the rules of several different organizations. There's quite a lot of convergence, but still a lot of differences too. If you ride Race Across America, you can use several bikes – a time trial bike, a climbing bike, a nice comfy one for the last few hours. If you want to set a Guinness World Record, you have to use the same bike all the way. If you ride the World 24-hour Championships,* which runs near San Diego every November, your support crew can't leave a designated pit area. Even if there's a problem, the rider has to get an official vehicle back to the pit. If you ride the UK 24-hour Championships, the crew can come and help you anywhere on the course. Different races and organizations expect different standards of timing and tracking, have different regulations about following vehicles. In a pro version of the sport, teams and riders would expect much more consistency so that they can use the same equipment and approach, and don't keep getting caught out because they'd turned up with the wrong colour reflective tape on their

---

* It's not recognized as a Championship by the World Ultra Cycling Association, but it's still broadly accepted as an event. It's like the early days of Victorian cycling when anyone who fancied calling their race a World Champs just went ahead and did so.

wheels. And they'd want consistent refereeing, so you'd need to create a large number of umpires and decide how they were going to operate and what colour blazer they'd wear.

'I can see it happening at some point in ultra racing,' Kemper told me. 'But you probably need to get 50 people round a table somewhere to agree the rules. And they're not even going to start off from a common conception of what ultra racing is supposed to be.' For some races it's a very straight competition. For others it's an expression of a certain view of the world and a cyclist's place within it. Some races would insist on a no-fly rule, others would regard that as the stupidest thing they'd ever heard.

You could even argue that at the moment the sport is going in the opposite direction. The idea of Fastest Known Time (FKT) records means you can work on the basis of not much more than a GPS tracker like Strava. There are some websites that record the best times, but there's nothing very formal at all and the website owners aren't setting themselves up as a governing body. There is no entry fee, no notifications, and no officials or timekeepers to deal with. You just do the ride, send your GPS evidence to a website and claim it. It's not even totally clear you need to do that – if you got a news website to publish the story widely enough, that would probably do. It's the absolute opposite of something like the Road Records Association (RRA), which regulates place-to-place records in the UK and remains a glory of Victorian bureaucracy. It's telling that the North Coast 500, a 500-mile circuit in the North of Scotland, has seen several men's FKT records set over the last few years, while the equivalent RRA record for the same route has not seen an initial men's mark even set. (There is a women's mark, set by End-to-End record holder Christina Mackenzie in 2022.) An RRA record has more official gravity, and you get awarded a nice red cycling cap, but a lot of riders are happy with the unofficial version.

Of course, there might be some upsides to the cash riders. The amateur sport is accessible only to those that can pay for it. That's hugely limiting for long supported races or records, which need either deep pockets or sponsors, and for individual riders sponsors are hard to find and nearly as hard to satisfy. For unsupported races there's not quite the same pressure, but as an amateur you still have major time commitment. Quite honestly that points you to certain sorts of employment, and ideally limited family obligations. (Or, 'Don't employ an ultra rider, and never ever marry one.')

A professional element might at least be more meritocratic in terms of who gets to compete at the top level – ability would matter more. If the sport keeps growing, and the interest in it keeps increasing, it's only a matter of time. But there would be a lot of current riders and organizers, perhaps even most of them, who'd be sorry to see the end of the current anarchic, varied, patchwork sport.

7

Fifteen Minutes, the Perfect Night's Sleep

The single most overwhelming thing about an ultra race or record attempt is simply that the clock never stops ticking. And it ticks most loudly when you're not moving.

Sometimes there's no real choice. You have to stop if you need to fix a puncture, or to put on or take off (most) items of clothing as the weather changes. You have to stop to buy food on an unsupported race, and your only real debate is over this shop or the next shop. But sometimes there is a choice, and the most optional-feeling stop of all is for sleep. Never will you feel more like a race is heading over the horizon without you than when you're stationary simply to take a rest. You might be unconscious but that doesn't mean you're not still racing flat out, and this tension never goes away.

Under the circumstances it's not surprising that there is a certain amount of machismo about sleeping. Riders who wouldn't dream of bragging about the time they forgot to eat for six hours and passed out as a result will take positive delight in telling you about the time they rode for 72 hours without stopping and ended up hallucinating that a roadside coffee shop was full of crocodiles in top hats. (A genuine hallucination, by the way.)

Happily and unhappily, in a 24-hour race you don't sleep at all. If you're getting it right, you barely even stop at all. Before my first 24-hour I was very doubtful about this part of it. To make it worse, the UK Championship race doesn't even start till around 2 p.m., which means that by the time you finish you've been awake for around 30 hours.

To my surprise, though, sleep didn't even make the top 10 list of things that I've ended up worrying about in these races. Staying awake is a piece of cake. In my first 24-hour I put this down to a monumental caffeine intake – it ended up being bolstered by the switch to energy gels in the second half, most of which had caffeine in them because that was all we had brought on an assumption that they'd only be used as an occasional pick-me-up. I also had a raging desire to drink tea in preference to any of the more appropriate liquids.

In 24 hours I consumed something over 1,200 mg of caffeine, the rough equivalent of 20 double espressos, which was way more than planned. Caffeine used to be banned by the doping authorities over a certain level, but incredibly I'd still probably have been under the historical limit. It's hard to work out the levels in your system just from the consumption, but I think I'd need to have consumed my 20 espressos in about half the time to fail the old test.

In my next 24-hour the caffeine intake was a fraction of that, no more than about 300 mg. I still stayed awake without any difficulty. Historically there are instances of riders in 24-hour events falling asleep on the bike and crashing, but I don't think I know anyone it's happened to. There are lots of problems with that length of race, but falling asleep doesn't seem to be a regular one.

I asked Dr Charlotte Elsworth-Edelsten about sleeping in ultra events. She's a sleep specialist with a background in human biomechanics and neurology, whose research in the area started out 20 years ago looking at the relationship between sleep and movement in stroke patients, before moving into studying sleep and athletes, especially athletes in long events. Inevitably I found myself thinking of her as 'Dr Sleep'. Sometimes, writing a book like this, you find yourself talking to someone who knows a vast amount about a topic on which you know next to nothing, and it's always a treat.

She's done a lot of work with ultra runners at events like the Ultra Trail de Mont Blanc (UTMB), a 170-km trail race usually won in around 20–26 hours. (Most athletes take longer – the time cutoff is 46 hours, so for most it's two nights out of bed. About 60% of starters finish inside the cut – it's not an event for the casual entrant.) There she recruits test subjects in exchange for running her own aid stations for them. And she's worked with athletes on altogether longer events and records.

'We fit runners with accelerometers,' she told me. 'We can track sleep before and during the races. We came into this knowing that sleep helps with movement, but the idea was to try to quantify it. So with our athletes we do a psychomotor vigilance test, which looks at reaction times, we ask about hallucinations, we check what stimulants they might be using – usually caffeine, but not always – and we offer them the chance to sleep somewhere reasonably nice. We do another reaction time test a kilometre further on to deal with any issues of sleep latency. The question is whether people who sleep more deal with everything better than those who sleep less.'

I liked the way she organizes the 'hotel' function of her trail-side gazebos. 'They lie down, we put a blanket over them, which helps block out any light and noise. Often we have quite a few athletes under blankets, so normally we stick a Post-it note to the blanket on their head telling us when to wake them up and send them off.'

She is clear that how long you sleep is critical. In a short event, like the Mont Blanc event, athletes should be sleeping for no longer than about 15 minutes. The range she aims for with subjects is 13–17 minutes. This is short enough to make sure that they don't enter a deep-sleep phase – waking from deep sleep is disorienting and really not very pleasant. It's the same territory and justification as the 'power nap'. You don't even necessarily need to sleep. What she describes as 'deep rest' is almost as good, just 15 minutes under a blanket.

Short naps work surprisingly well. The Elsworth-Edelsten take is that for events of anything up to a few days they ought to be enough for anyone who is competing seriously. They work because there are two reasons we need to sleep. The first is basic circadian rhythm – daylight wakes you up, darkness makes you sleep. 'The way you feel terrible at 3 a.m., and 90 minutes later when the sun comes up you immediately feel better,' was how she put it.

The other part of the process is that from the moment you wake up from a normal night's sleep, there is a build up of homeostatic sleep pressure – an increasing level of chemicals that effectively apply pressure to sleep, like someone very gradually squeezing on the brakes. You dissipate it completely with a good night's sleep, but you can relieve a certain amount of the pressure with a short nap.

The mechanisms behind all this are not clear, but the results are. The metabolism in the muscles is improved, the oxygen costs of exercise are reduced. Sleeping makes you a better athlete. 'At a practical level,' says Elsworth-Edelsten, 'you watch someone arrive at the aid stations exhausted, dragging their feet. They sleep for 13 minutes, and leave looking very different.' When they compare exhausted runners who sleep versus exhausted runners who don't, it's clear that the time lost sleeping is recovered. 'I think the rule is to sleep when you feel like you need it, just treat it symptomatically,' she says. 'We often see runners at UTMB who really feel the fatigue hit hard just after the sun comes up. But it's better to sleep at night if you can.

'There would be times when you just have to crack on, like you're a few kilometres from a cutoff and are barely going to make it. But otherwise, you should be incorporating some sleep when you feel you need it,' she said.

For something like Land's End to John O'Groats, in the two-day bracket, riders more often than not push through the first night – call it macho, call it tradition, or call it trying to work off the current record holder's progress. Elsworth-Edelsten is convinced that's a mistake. 'A 15 minute on night one would be a really good idea,' she says. 'Even if you don't feel like you need it, it has a prophylactic effect. There are real benefits to it. Then night two, maybe the same again, or maybe even a little bit longer – you can go to 30 minutes without getting into deep sleep, so perhaps you'd go to that on night two.'

I can see why people don't take the advice – 30–45 minutes asleep feels like a long time in a race that's less than two days long. Put it another way, it might be 15 miles' worth. You need to be more than a third of a mile per hour faster over the rest of the ride to catch up with it. On an intuitive level, it's wrong. When Mike Broadwith broke the End-to-End record in 2018, he didn't sleep at any point in the 43 hours, and that coming after an interrupted and nervous night's sleep before the start. Most End-to-End riders historically have tried to do it that way, and perhaps succumbed to a short nap somewhere on night two.

(The women's record is harder from the perspective of sleep, since they'd have a full second night to get through – a male record breaker would typically finish around 2–3 a.m., but a woman breaking the current record – 51 hours, set by Christina Mackenzie in 2021 – wouldn't finish till 9 or 10 a.m. the next day.)

There's also an anxiety about stopping. 'If I stopped I worry that I'd never start again,' is something that several people said to me, including Broadwith. Spine Race runner Mark Turner told me that he even avoided sleeping

FIFTEEN MINUTES, THE PERFECT NIGHT'S SLEEP

in the aid stations because they were too comfortable: 'I'd sleep in a bag on the trail, because it was easier to get up and go again.' (Although, he also pointed out that he usually reached aid stations in daylight, and in a race held in midwinter sleeping didn't seem like a good use of daylight.)

But I also appreciate what a long way down an ultra racing rabbit hole you are when someone suggests sleeping for 45 minutes over two nights, and you suck your teeth and complain that that seems a little indulgent. If it were me, I'd sleep, because my experience of nearly every analogous intuition versus actual science clash in 25 years as a bike racer has been that the science is closer to the right answer than whatever you intuitively think.

There is also the question of how you sleep. I had a conversation at a race with someone who'd been part of a RAAM crew, looking after a British rider. 'I saw a video of Christoph Strasser stopping for a sleep,' he said. 'And it was incredible. He'd stop on the road shoulder, the crew would already have a mat and a blanket down. He'd just immediately lie down and go to sleep. The crew would service the bike, quietly. Fifteen minutes later they'd wake him up, he'd get straight on the bike and go. His 15 minutes asleep cost him around 16 minutes of riding. The rider I was looking after was probably not much slower than Strasser when they were actually on the bike. But at a sleep stop, they'd get off, have a chat, debate where we should put the mat, lie down, talk to us some more about how it was going. Eventually they'd have a sleep, then get up, have another chat, have some food and drink sitting there rather than eat it on the go… a 15-minute sleep took about 40 minutes.' Over a week-long race, that rapidly adds up to half a day.

I repeated this to Strasser. He told me, 'Maybe 45 minutes before I stop, I have a chat with the team on the radio. We talk about everything that we need to do – to the bike, whether I want different clothes, anything like that. Then at 30 minutes to the stop, I stop the talk. I start to relax as I ride, to get ready for the sleep, and I start to feel a bit sleepy. Maybe it's a bit like a meditation? Then when I stop, I'm already prepared for sleep, so I can lie down and be asleep as quickly as possible.'

The reason for the 15-minute nap is to avoid deep sleep. But you can only sustain that for so long. As races get longer, the approach needs to change. For a week-long race like RAAM most racers are probably somewhere at the very fringes of being able to manage on 15-minute naps. You probably ought to sleep for longer at points, especially towards the end. It maybe becomes a more efficient way to do it anyway, as the frequency of the naps you need to get by starts to increase.

Riders doing supported events lasting into a second week, like a longer record attempt, or on any substantial unsupported race where self-care is more of a priority, need to start sleeping longer from an early point in the race. A light-sleep/deep-sleep cycle usually takes around 90 minutes to complete. So the tri-modal distribution of sleeping duration is 15 minutes (maybe up to 30, but certainly no more), then all the way to at least 90 minutes. Beyond 90 minutes, you get straight to three hours and sleep two cycles. If you're trying to be competitive, you're not usually going to sleep for any longer.

'The general rule is that on a long event, you need to sleep for three hours out of any 24,' says Elsworth-Edelsten. You can do that by two nineties, one three-hour, or a combination of longer sleeps and short naps. And of course, ultimately it depends a bit on what you're at the event for. If you're determined to compete at the front, you'll probably sleep less. If your main aim is just to complete it within a time cut, you're a lot more likely to manage that without a total meltdown if you sleep a bit more. That's not least because if your average speed when you're awake is lower, you lose less distance/time when you're asleep.

(As an aside, it interests me that the centuries-old watch-keeping pattern on ships and racing yachts is four hours on, four hours off, which allows nicely for a three-hour sleep. This is clearly not a coincidence.)

There are some riders who go a different way. Leigh Timmis's strategy for his European side-to-side record (a 16-day ride) was to sleep for seven hours a night in a tent beside the team RV, more than double the amount most riders would expect to get. The intention was to get the time back by riding faster through being better rested. But part of the reasoning for this was that he was very unsure about how long the record would take. 'It could have been 20 days,' he told me. 'So we attempted to come up with a strategy that could be sustained indefinitely. In the end I didn't really ever get a full seven hours anyway, and if I was doing it again I'd focus more on quality of sleep rather than quantity.' In a subsequent seven-day record attempt, he cut sleep back to five hours, and back again to three in the closing stages.

In the end, though, most riders sleep a lot less, frequently even less than Elsworth-Edelsten's suggestion. In the racing moment, there is every reason not to stop. In races like TCR, a race tactic that more than one rider referred to was simply to race through the first night, and race through the second until all of your rivals had stopped for a sleep. Only then did you stop yourself, have a short nap, and go again. Then all you needed to do was sleep only when everyone else had slept, and you'd always be in front.

This is clearly true, even if it's almost impossible to put into practice. What is pretty clear is that the riders at the front of a race field spend more time awake than the ones in the middle. It's difficult to get accurate numbers on it, but the GPS tracking for events shows the percentage of time riders spend moving. As a general rule, serious riders on things like TCR are moving at least 80% of the time. At the very front of the field, it's closer to 85%. Which means they would be stationary for an average of less than four hours a day. Given that also includes food shopping, crossing borders and fixing any punctures or mechanicals (and on TCR, which has compulsory gravel sections, there are quite a few punctures for most riders), it's clear that three hours' sleep a day is going to be towards the top end of what's possible.

In the 2024 TCR, the men's winner, Robin Gemperle, was moving 82% of the time; Christoph Strasser in second was moving 85% but covered a little more distance. Riders in the teens were generally around the mid-70s. Riders in the 20-something positions were more often in the mid-60s – though there does start to be more variability as different strategies begin to make more sense. The proportion doesn't really drop much more than that – generally at the back of the field riders are still riding 60% of the time, or around 15 hours a day; they're just going more slowly. This is a trend that broadly repeats across other editions of the race. Shorter races have (unsurprisingly) higher moving proportions, and simpler races (fewer border crossings, fewer gravel sections) also have higher moving proportions.

Supported riders often try to get by on even less sleep – maybe just a couple of naps a day to start with, gradually increasing as the race goes on. They've got less need to plan, because they've got the facilities available to sleep at any time. They also don't have to look after themselves – they've got a team on the radio to say 'Look out at the junction' or 'There's a town in five miles, so better rest now' or even just chatter to the rider and keep them engaged in the world. 'In RAAM, essentially the crew end up nursing a bad-tempered, exhausted toddler across a continent,' was how Shu Pillinger put it. She slept no more than a couple of hours a day on RAAM, but somewhat more on TCR. RAAM winners often sleep for no more than an average of an hour a day.

As well as the mental toll, and the physiological degradation of lack of sleep, there are other effects. It's probably not a huge exaggeration to say that there are two sorts of ultra athlete: those who have experienced a hallucination brought on by lack of sleep, and those who are jealous of them. I've only experienced one, and it wasn't even while cycling, it was during a week-long sailing race. Around dawn one morning, I saw a fleet of other boats heading in the opposite direction, clearly nothing to do with the race I was in. I pointed them out to a crewmate, and said, 'I wonder what race that is.' He looked baffled. 'That fleet over there,' I said. 'With the spinnakers up. Right there.' I could see them long after I'd been assured that they didn't exist. There was a reality to them, and a lack of any dream-like quality.

Ultra runner Mark Turner has experienced several hallucinations in his racing. 'Normally it would be on the second night of a race, when the fatigue is beginning to build. One night I saw a huge woolly mammoth sleeping beside the trail,' he told me. 'And I looked at it and thought that would be just a lovely warm, cuddly place to curl up for a sleep, just in the fur of its belly.' Sadly for Mark and for palaeontologists everywhere, the mammoth didn't exist. When he got there it was just a tree. 'I've seen trees as goblins at a race in Ireland, and wolves and dogs snarling by the trail,' he says. 'And I've seen other people having hallucinations. On the Spine Race I came round a corner and there was a huge Polish runner punching the hell out of a rock, over and over, shouting, "They're going to get me." He was really freaked out, his hands were bleeding. I stopped him and helped him to the next feed station. He was really gone, he just had a thousand-yard stare.'

Shu Pillinger also has considerable experience of things that aren't there. 'It's pretty scary at first, because you've no idea what they are. Then you start to not trust things that are actually real, because you don't know the difference. On my second RAAM I began to understand a bit more, even interact with them, and start to know what's real and what's not. But sometimes I'd still do something like turn off the road, and the crew would be on the radio saying, "What are you doing, where are you going?" I'd say, "You told me to turn off," and they'd tell me the turn wasn't for another 100 miles.'

It's probably not surprising that my expert witness on sleeping, Charlotte Elsworth-Edelsten, is not a fan of the hallucination as a mid-race distraction. 'People really crave them. But they're a danger sign, it's your brain beginning to shut down.' Sadly, they really mean you ought to back off a bit, have a nap, and wake up stronger.

Given the importance of sleep, the obvious question is whether there's any useful training you can do. After all, you can train everything else, pretty much. It's what athletes do when faced with something difficult. When Mick Coupe broke the Land's End to John O'Groats record in 1982 (a record that lasted just six weeks before being bested by John Woodburn's 'three meals a day' ride), part of his training consisted of skipping a night's sleep twice a week during his months of training. That didn't stop his brutal riding schedule, which often involved two hours' riding before work (frequently after a night awake) and another five hours afterwards.

In general, the consensus is that it's something you can't really train. There is an extent to which you can perhaps get used to the effects of sleep deprivation, to learn what it's going to feel like and just how deep a hole you can dig. But it seems that when it comes to sleep, you can't really move back the boundaries of what you can tolerate by pushing against them in training.

Part of your problem is that if, like Coupe, you knock sleeping on the head, you severely compromise your recovery from the other training. Even if you could increase your ability to stay awake by, say, 30 minutes a day, the 6–10 miles that might gain you would probably be wiped out by the drop in sustainable power – though of course it would vary by individual.

In practice a lot of what Elsworth-Edelsten does when she works with an athlete isn't quite what you'd expect. Through the preparation and training phase what she does is not so much to do with dealing with sleep deprivation in the race, it's more to do with maximizing sleep and recovery. 'Over three or four months I'd work to improve their basic sleep,' she says. 'Some athletes have a major race in three months, a race they've maybe been working their way towards for a couple of years, and they are sleeping five hours a night. They're going to bed at one in the morning, drinking coffee all evening. Sometimes it's really low-hanging fruit, just helping with some basic sleep hygiene.'

So it's all the stuff you already know about, which athletes are sometimes terrible at applying to themselves. Get to bed at a sensible time. Make sure you have a dark, quiet bedroom. Don't drink coffee late in the day. If you do nothing but increase the amount of sleep you're getting, that's still enough to start with. If it doesn't feel as if it has a lot to do with staying awake for a week somewhere down the line, well, it probably doesn't, not directly. But it's one of the ways you make yourself faster when you're moving, so perhaps it gives you a bit more time to sleep and you net out in front. Sleep is performance-enhancing, and that's never a bad thing.

'It's about improving sleep quality, and sleep efficiency,' she says. 'How long are you in bed, and how much of the time are you sleeping? It's like pizza dough, you need to stretch the sleep out without tearing holes in it, without spending time lying awake in the middle of the night worrying about things.' A lot of this feels very basic, but athletes still can't be relied upon to get it right. 'There are lots of things we can do,' she says. 'We can look at melatonin responses, cortisol release, phases of sleep. But there's no point in doing any of it until the fundamentals are right.'

The other element to Elsworth-Edelsten's work is dealing with specific sleep issues, like athletes who struggle to sleep because of anxiety or stress in the build up – very common with record attempts because usually the athlete bears a lot of the organizational burden. And there may be other specific sleep issues if an athlete is training or planning to race at altitude, something that almost invariably leads to disturbed sleep and even altitude-induced sleep apnoea.

'All of this takes a long time,' she says. 'If you called me and said you were doing an ultra race next week, there's not a lot I can do. If you're going to bed at 1 a.m., there's not much point in me telling you to start going to bed at 9 p.m. right now.'

Almost the only race-specific intervention that Elsworth-Edelsten mentions is periodization of sleep. That's shifting the hours that you sleep to fit in with the time of competition. In some ways it's a more obvious thing to do for something like a middle distance race that starts very early in the morning, like an Iron Man triathlon. If you shift your sleep from, say, 10 p.m.–6 a.m. to 8 p.m.–4 a.m., it would give you a better chance of being ready for a 7 a.m. start.

It can also be relevant for an ultra, though, if the ultra starts very early or late. Typical start times for a Land's End to John O'Groats ride are 6–8 a.m. Start times for some races are 8–10 p.m., to plunge you straight into darkness and maybe help you get through at least one night reasonably fresh. You might find an advantage to pushing your sleep back a little later, which at least means you haven't been awake for 12 or 13 hours before you even start.

The other thing you can do is use some form of stimulant. Caffeine is the main one, and certainly the main legal one in a race that's subject to anti-doping provisions. It's cheap, readily available, easy to consume and something that it's not hard to experiment with even outside a race. At a basic empirical level you can get a feel for your tolerance, your response, how quickly it absorbs and starts to kick in, whether it produces any gut issue when you combine it with big carbohydrate intakes – all of which vary considerably from individual to individual.

And in a long race, strategically deployed, for most people it can make a real difference. A big climb at 2 a.m.? It will help with that. Sleepiness at a point where you really don't want to stop because you'll miss a time cut, or because the finish isn't all that far away? It will help with that. The best results usually come not from taking huge quantities consistently all day and all night, but using it to hit the hard bits and the low bits.

It's not going to stop you sleeping when you need to, because if you're the sort of tired that riders get in really long races, you're the sort of tired that caffeine won't easily defeat. You might not want to take 600 mg at midnight if you're getting to a hotel at 1.30 a.m. for a three-hour stop, but outside of that kind of excess, it's unlikely to be an issue.

Traditional wisdom had it that abstaining from caffeine before an event enhanced the effects. To some extent it does, but Elsworth-Edelsten points out a risk: 'The highs will be higher, but the comedown will be more dramatic. If you don't take caffeine for a few weeks, then you take 300 mg in a race, the effects will probably be heightened. But that post-caffeine crash will be magnified too. So then you need more caffeine to deal with that, and there's a vicious circle. It would be safer to modulate your caffeine intake than to just eliminate it.'

If I accept (and I do) that you can't really train for it, I also have to accept that not everyone is created equal when it comes to their ability to deal with sleep deprivation. It's individual, and it's not related especially closely to the other aspects of being an athlete. Some elite athletes simply don't function on limited sleep, even in short events like a 24-hour. It's not even necessarily that they can't stay awake, it's the effects on your physiology that the pressure to sleep produces. As Dr Elsworth-Edelsten has observed, tired and sleep-deprived runners are not fast runners, and this impact is not the same for everyone.

Others seem much less affected by it. But it's not simple to predict who is who. 'The chances are that if you sleep 10 hours a night and need a bit of a lie-in, you're not going to be the right person to win RAAM or TCR,' she says. 'On the other hand, maybe if you're the sort of person who's a bit highly strung, maybe a bit obsessive-compulsive, who perhaps doesn't sleep a huge amount anyway, that seems to be the right sort of person. I can often see trends, but you can't ever be quite certain.'

She also pointed out that, actually, rather a lot of athletes fit that personality profile pretty well – and I'd agree that there are almost certainly more of them among athletes than there are 10-hours-a-night, laid-back loafers.

Some people are better at delaying sleep, or at least being flexible about exactly when they need to sleep. When trans-Europe record breaker Leigh Timmis rode his first TCR, switching to an unsupported event, his original plan was to stop from midnight to four in the morning every day, to try to keep the circadian rhythm consistent. This is good science. The problem he found with it was that the circumstances of the race often fell at odds with it. 'Next time I'd allocate sleep around geographical or technical challenges,' he told me. 'Next time I'd approach it by understanding the needs of each parcours [a compulsory section of route you're required to cover – normally gravel] and structure the sleep to make sure I arrived at those in daylight and as fresh as possible. Midnight to four meant I ended up spending a lot of time neither asleep nor moving, and didn't sleep very well.'

For most riders sleeping is one of the highlights of an ultra. Almost everyone talks about a precious few moments as you wake up as you hover between awake and asleep, in a deep and unique peace with the world that only exhaustion and a little relief from it can produce. Somewhere you know that much too soon you'll have to get back on the bike, and that when that happens, for at least a few minutes till you warm up and loosen out, you're going to feel as terrible as you ever have in your life.

Occasionally it can even border on magical. Emily Chappell told me about being overcome with tiredness one night in the mountains, and finding a safe place to sleep in a field just off the road. When she woke, it was daylight. She was in an Alpine meadow, surrounded by wild flowers under a blue, blue sky, with high mountains in the distance. For a few moments, it was very close to perfection.

Then she got up and got back on her bike.

8

A Perfect Equilibrium of Discomfort

Cyclists like bikes, at least most of the time. Clearly bikes are wilful objects, and most of us have had occasion to curse them; a handful of us have hurled them into hedges in a rage and then had the undignified experience of having to go and retrieve them, rather than have them crawl back apologetically on their own which is what you somehow expect. But for the most part, we're fans. In a way, the occasional deranged disagreement with a bike serves to show how intimate the relationship is. We are cyclists, and without a bike we would be pedestrians, or worse, bystanders.

This relationship is all the stronger for an ultra rider. If you're doing something like TCR or RAAM, the bike is the main constant in your life. It's where you live for weeks at a time. I spoke to one TCR rider who said that after a few days he found it almost impossible to leave his bike outside a shop while he ran in to get food because his fear of it being stolen had passed the rational end-of-his-race/expensive-replacement zone of thinking, and become something profoundly emotional. The thought of losing it was just too big a concept to deal with.

The nature of the right bike for an ultra is different from a shorter race. Reliability matters more. Comfort matters more. Adaptability becomes important for some races, where a bike has to cope with multiple surfaces and riding styles. On the other hand, outright performance matters less. Weight and aerodynamics have a less obvious influence on the outcome than they would do in a Tour de France stage when so much of everything else is so tightly controlled – though I'd argue that it's not so much that they're less important as that the way you look at and assess them is a little different. The weight and aerodynamics of your bike frame matter less when you've covered it in bike-packing bags, but that just means the weight and aerodynamics of the bags become something you might want to pay attention to.

There's also the question of what you take with you, either on the bike or with a support crew. For unsupported riders, the choices are almost endless, and the luggage of a TCR rider is so fascinating that the standard issue pre-race interview is, more often than not, about what they're taking with them – perhaps with photos of everything laid out. It's not as superficial as it sounds. Your equipment tells a whole story about your expectations, even your personality.

The race itself matters. Beyond the basic bifurcation of supported versus unsupported, there's the route. Does it have gravel sections? How much climbing? How far from civilization does it go?

What governing body you're racing under can matter. If you're trying to break a Guinness World Record, you have to ride the same bike the whole way, even if you have a support crew. If you're doing RAAM, you can change to a climbing bike for the hills, and back to a more aerodynamic bike for the flats.

Above all, there's the question of what the event is. When I asked multiple RAAM and TCR winner Christoph Strasser about equipment choices, he said a lot of it was about balancing speed versus comfort versus aero. 'For RAAM, it is about comfort. In RAAM the things that stop you are things that hurt, like your neck, your hands and fingers – though the ability to change bikes means you can tune the balance as you go. For TCR, carrying everything on the bike over that long, it's about weight. For a 24-hour record, it is so short that comfort doesn't matter. But it's relatively fast, so it's all about aerodynamics.'

In some ways this wasn't a helpful thing for someone to say to me while I was planning for a 24-hour race. I've never really found bikes to be especially comfortable things, and I envy people who seem able to easily become one with their machine. I haven't found a saddle that doesn't rub somewhere, or leave me shuffling back and forth looking for a sweet spot that feels like it should be there somewhere, but remains always out of reach.

But Strasser's casual mention of 'speed' means aerodynamics, and I do know something about that. I've spent several years running a consultancy that provides aero testing for bike riders. Over many hours at the controls of a wind tunnel, I've learned how much aerodynamics matters, even at relatively modest ultra rider speeds, and how very individual it is. And also the difficulty of reconciling aerodynamics and comfort. The most important factor for bike aerodynamics is not the bike, but the position of the rider on it. The fastest riding positions are low, with your head tucked right down. Riding like that is, as Strasser implied, the opposite of comfortable.

It pulls you forwards on the bike, so there's too much weight on your arms and shoulders. It strains your neck as you try to keep your head low yet look where you're going. And your shoulders are getting on towards being level with your hips. That rotates your pelvis forwards so that it's difficult to put your weight on the saddle through your sit bones – you end up sitting on soft tissue that has not been adequately designed for the purpose.

It's liveable with for short time trials, but it produces issues on long rides. There is always a compromise between a full-on, aerodynamically focused 'time trial' position, the sort of thing you develop in a wind tunnel with few concessions to comfort, and a 'road bike' position, where you sit up higher above the bars, in a more relaxed, more conventional position. You need different bikes to do the different extremities of the spectrum. Time trial bikes have stiff, responsive frames that are not all that comfortable because they transmit road shock to the saddle. Road bikes are more forgiving all round, but they're slower. In the middle of the spectrum, various compromises are possible, usually by putting aero bar extensions on a road bike.

A PERFECT EQUILIBRIUM OF DISCOMFORT

For the 24-hour races I was very much at the time trial extremity. I was using a new (well, third-hand new) time trial bike of the full-on variety. I bought it before the bright idea of riding it all day and all night occurred to me; I had originally been planning to use it for not much more than the odd local race. I'd set it up as closely as I could to my previous bike, and made a few aerodynamic position tweaks based on my experience of wind tunnel testing other people – I made my position a little shorter and more compact, and changed the angle of the aero bars to get my hands close to my face. I got a new helmet that I'd seen test well on several riders, and a new race suit.

All of this was no better than educated guesswork because, while I'd run wind tunnel testing for quite a lot of other people, it was years since I'd been on a bike in a tunnel myself. And in the world of aero, the emphasis would be on the 'guesswork' not the 'educated'. As a branch of cycling, aerodynamics is not just rider specific, it's weirdly specific. A helmet that's phenomenally fast on one rider can be an utter disaster on another. Same with suits, even if the two riders are similar in size and shape. Some riders are faster if they put a bottle on the bike. Some are slower. Some are faster in long socks, some in short. You get the idea. And the differences can quickly stack up into a couple of kilometres an hour. If you really want to know how much drag a position generates, you have to measure it. And measuring it is either expensive, like the wind tunnel, or laborious, like field testing on the open road.

For sure, you can get proper aero data out on the road, and I've done it in the past. But it requires hours and hours of testing, and some very inconvenient practices. The search for ideal conditions (no more than a light wind, absolutely zero traffic) led to a week of testing a few years ago up and down a local road between 1 and 4 a.m. Over five nights and 15 hours I managed to get solid data on two skinsuits and some shaky data on two helmets. Also, three near-collisions with deer, and one completely freaked-out passer-by who, when my bright, bright lights approached at 30 mph in total silence thought the rapture was upon him.

Frankly I'm 10 years older now than I was when I did that, and my patience has diminished. As a testing method it was cheap and it was accessible but it was approaching being a full-time job.

When the 24-hour idea started to become a real thing, I decided to do the job properly. I booked some time in a wind tunnel, and the services of Bianca Broadbent, a physio and very experienced bike fitter. I decided that the 24-hour campaign was where I would finally begin again from the start and find a position that was sustainable, even if it gave away a little in terms of speed.

I was especially interested in Bianca's side of this equation, which was the comfort and biomechanics side, which I almost ignored for my whole career as I pursued the aero elements. My existing saddle height dated from when I was a student and I bought a second-hand Lotus time trial bike that had a non-adjustable seat post – the post was just part of the monocoque and the idea was you sawed it to length with a hacksaw and bolted a saddle clamp to the top. I was too scared to cut the thing properly. I took a bit off it, leaving some random centimetre or two of spare length as a precaution, installed the saddle at whatever random height I'd ended up with, and never questioned it again. I diligently transferred it from bike to bike for the next 20 years. The rest of the position was either a plain guess, or based on tunnel testing from a decade previously. There was no presiding intelligence behind this whatsoever. If I'd thought you were a bit gullible, I might have tried to describe it as evolution. In practice I'd accept that it was closer to negligence.

Bianca set my bike up on a home trainer on a rotating platform, in a sport science lab we'd borrowed from Birmingham University – it was a postscript to a day I'd spent doing physiology tests for a friend's research. She set up three cameras on tripods, and stuck several fluorescent markers to various key bits of me so that her cameras could capture a 3D image of me pedalling and read all the limb and joint angles. I rode the bike, and every so often Bianca rotated the whole platform with me on it so she could capture different viewpoints. The process took several minutes.

I'd expected a sharp intake of breath and a lot of changes. Instead, she invited me to look at the screen, showing a stick-figure me with all the joint angles tracked. 'It's not bad,' she said. 'If you were new to cycling, there are some things I'd change. But the thing is, you've been doing this a long time in this position. It's probably not "perfect", but it seems to work OK, so I'm going to leave most of it. You could put your saddle down 10 mm if you like, but that's really about it.' When I reported this to a former coach, he just said, 'She's right. You're an old horse.'

The other thing we did in the session was put a pressure-sensitive pad on my saddle, and look for pressure points. We worked through several saddles with this, looking for an optimum. In the end we never really found one, and ended up deciding an old saddle that I'd taken off my winter bike to try at the session was probably as good as anything. It was fairly flat-topped, which I seem to suit, and it didn't have a hole in the middle like practically every current saddle on the market – the pressure mapping showed that the main effect for me of a hole was to dramatically increase the pressure created around its sides.

None of this had made any miraculous difference in comfort, but the increments all added up. And at least it was enough to stop me continually fiddling around for the next few weeks till the race, in search of something that wasn't attainable. Perhaps everyone else is no more comfortable than I am, it's just that they complain less.

It's also worth thinking about the way the concept of comfort changes over time. For a short ride, it's just about feeling good. For a very long ride, well, it's not going to feel good in quite the same way, whatever you do. The issue becomes one of avoiding anything becoming so painful it actually stops you. Bianca suggested that if you get it right, everything hurts the same, and nothing breaches your defences. You are in a perfect equilibrium of discomfort.

Of course, if this was literally what you'd managed, when it went wrong everything would go wrong at exactly the same moment. The implosion would be total, and probably instantaneous.

A PERFECT EQUILIBRIUM OF DISCOMFORT

One of the things I was dealing with was a lower back that had been very unreliable over the previous year. I could make a saddle more comfortable by tilting the nose down a little, but at the cost of making my back hurt a bit more. The advice was simple. You're a lot more likely to be stopped by a sore back than by a sore arse. You can survive a lot of saddle discomfort, because it's exactly the kind of pain you can ignore in reasonable safety, and it's more or less independent of the level of effort. Back pain or knee pain is proportionate to how hard you try. Saddle discomfort isn't.

Something else that Bianca did do for me was make a pair of custom insoles for my bike shoes. They were stunningly good. 'Hot foot' is one of the big problems riders have in long events, and one I had in every 12-hour I rode. It's the sensation of stabbing-hot, painful feet – and it can be very unpleasant indeed. I've seen riders who've ended up cutting away most of their shoes mid-race in an attempt to alleviate the symptoms by reducing the pressure and increasing the airflow, leaving a sole and just enough material to hold it to their feet.

In the subsequent 24-hour, I never once had cause to think about my feet. Even after I finished, they were fine.

After the session with Bianca, I went to the wind tunnel. There I was less than delighted to discover that all the changes I'd made on my new bike, the ones based on my long experience and deep accumulated wisdom, were largely wrong. I stretched the position out again, but avoided anything too radical and unsustainable. I looked at the aerodynamic penalty of some comfort-chasing compromises, like making it a little higher, or making my elbows 10 or 20 mm wider on the aero bars. Adding 10 mm on the bar height was, for instance, worth about 4 watts at 24-hour pace; 20 mm wider on the elbows was around the same. To me 4 watts felt like quite a lot – over the length of the race it would work out at about 8 km. In the end I stuck with something that was more on the aerodynamic side of the balance, probably because I was thinking of Christoph Strasser's ability to deal with discomfort rather than my own.

As usual, of course, it's the things you don't plan for. I had worked on the assumption that I'd be racing in the dry, and aero-tested suits accordingly. Come my first 24-hour and it was, as I may have mentioned, very much not dry. The race suit that I'd carefully tested in the tunnel spent more than half the race under a Gore-Tex rain jacket hastily borrowed from a member of the crew. It was an outstanding jacket from the point of view of keeping the rain out, but it was also quite flappy and it wasn't fast. I'd have felt like a bit of a Charlie testing rain jackets and jerseys in a wind tunnel, but it's exactly what I should have done.

The jacket was another trade-off – I knew it was slow for every moment I had it on. I could hear it rustling. For a 100-mile event it wouldn't have crossed my mind to wear it. But in a cold, wet 24-hour, the likely result of not using it would have been that I'd have ridden a kilometre an hour faster, right up to the point where I had to give up because I was getting hypothermic.

Overall, though, I was probably also a bit aggressive on the aero side of the balance. I'm a time trial rider by former profession, and I stuck a little too close to what

I understood best. By the last eight hours it got hard to stay in the aero tuck – I'd guess I spent half my time riding in a more upright position. Any excuse would do – uphill? Out of the tuck. Corner? Out of the tuck. Puddles and potholes? Out of the tuck. My lower back hurt, my shoulders hurt, and they were much easier to live with if I wasn't trying to stay folded up on the handlebars the whole time. The only thing that pushed the other way was a photographer – every time I saw one of those I made like Remco Evenepoel. Consequently all the available photographic evidence suggests I sustained a really good riding position to the bitter end, but I did not.

That issue is, of course, only partly one of pure position. There's a system at work – if I'd ridden less hard, I'd have sustained the position better because I'd have been less fatigued. It would have helped if the weather had been drier, because everything would have been a little easier, from seeing where I was going to the wretched wet chamois pad I was sitting on for most of the event. If I'd been less fatigued, I'd have been able to eat more. If I'd eaten more, I'd have had a bit more energy available. And so on. Christoph Strasser probably can sustain a more uncomfortable position than me, but part of it is his ability to get more of the other things right. In this, as in so many other bits of ultra riding, everything is connected to everything else.

In races longer than 24 hours, the balance shifts. How much it shifts depends on just how long. On a supported race, it might not shift all that much – Mike Broadwith's End-to-End set up was very similar to my 24-hour choices, and similar to the position he's used in the past for shorter races. It helped that he's better at this, and has more experience to back it up. He ran a bike that was a previous model of the one I used, with a full aero position, suit and helmet. He did spend a few hours on his spare bike when things got difficult, which was another time trial bike with a slightly less aggressive position. But other than the occasional extra jersey, at no point did he really look like he'd have been out of place at a 10-mile race. Partly that's the nature of record breaking. If he wasn't able to ride an aero position, he wasn't going to be fast enough to break the record, and if he wasn't going to break the record, he'd stop.

The issues I ended up dealing with were all relatively minor. They slowed me down somewhat, but they weren't going to end my ride. For riders who prioritize speed and aerodynamics, neck problems from the riding position are more common, and more serious. They can affect any riding set up, but it's especially acute for riders in supported events riding time trial bikes, because looking up to see the road from the low riding position exacerbates the unnatural position of your head and shoulders. Ultra riders live in fear of Shermer's Neck. It's named after Michael Shermer, who failed to finish the 1982 RAAM because his neck muscles could no longer support the weight of his head. In his End-to-End, Mike Broadwith ended up supporting his head with one hand on his chin and the elbow on the bars for most of the last nine hours of his ride.

Most solo rider RAAM crews carry a neck brace. Unsupported riders don't. In the TCR of 2015, James Hayden tried to improvise a strap out of tape to hold his head up – it attached a tape headband to a tape chest band.

It didn't work, and he was forced out agonizingly near the finish. Trying to analyse the issue afterwards, with a view to preventing it happening again, he concluded that the way to pre-empt it was a combination of bike fit and core strength, along with avoiding the 'everything else' problems of fatigue, lack of sleep and nutrition.

When you go longer than 24–48 hours, especially in races rather than records, things do start to move away from the pure time trial model. For a supported race, there's a wide spread. The fast riders will aim to ride a time trial-esque set up, at least for as long as they can manage, but almost invariably it's a bit de-tuned. The aero bars are set up higher and wider, because as the duration goes up and the speed goes down they start to be less purely an aerodynamic element, and have to become a comfortable position to drop into.

It's not a coincidence that the first elbow-rest aero bar arrangement to achieve prominence anywhere was under a RAAM rider called Jim Elliot in the 1984 race. It was devised by Richard Bryne – inventor of quite a lot of bike-related stuff including the Speedplay pedal and the turbo trainer. It was aimed as much at comfort as at speed. He did this by placing elbow rests behind a pair of drop bars, at the same width and height as the brake hoods, so that Elliot could sustain what we'd now regard as an aerodynamic, level-forearm road bike position, but without needing to hold his weight on his triceps and shoulders. Across the flatlands of Kansas into a headwind it was so obviously faster that at least one of the riders he passed tried to bodge together a copy of it on the spot.

By the 1986 race, others had copied and improved the arrangement, putting the elbow rests on the bars and installing extensions forwards. The aero bar revolution really took off when Greg LeMond used a pair to win the 1989 Tour de France, but their start in life was plodding across Kansas into a 20 mph headwind.

There's another advantage to aero bars. Ian Walker, North-to-South Europe record holder, told me, 'They're really good if you want to use your phone for something. You can control the bike with your elbows, see the phone, and see where you're going, all at the same time. And they're a lot easier for unwrapping food. Anything where you need both hands, really.'

Exactly where on the time trial to road bike spectrum you set yourself up varies by distance, event and rider. Some riders will use a full-on time trial bike that's not much different from the one I used in the 24. Some put aero bars on a road bike, on the basis that the position they're after is so high that it's difficult to create it on a time trial bike that's designed for short races. Road bikes are also typically lighter and more configurable. You can carry more bottles, it's easy to install a top tube bag for food – even in supported races, riders usually end up riding alone for fairly long periods and all those gels have to go somewhere. Riders who set out on a time trial bike often switch to a road bike for climbing, and often as not stick with it when things start to hurt. Unsupported racers almost always opt for a road bike. They're easier to carry stuff on, they're easier to fix, and they're better all-rounders if you only have one bike. The aerodynamics is already pretty compromised by the baggage anyway, so you're not surrendering all that much on that side.

As the distance goes up, the clothing changes. For 24–48 hours of supported racing, skinsuits are fairly standard, and aero helmets. Beyond that there's usually a shift to jersey and shorts for a bit more comfort and better pockets, and the aero helmet gives way to a road helmet, which is better ventilated and (Shermer's Neck...) quite a lot lighter.

In events longer than about 48 hours, most riders go with spoked wheels front and back, rather than using a solid disc on the back. Like a road bike over a time trial bike, spoked wheels are a little lighter, and while in purely engineering terms the aero advantage of a disc would outweigh that, they are also a bit more compliant to ride. A lot of modern discs, though, have a construction that's actually a spoked wheel with carbon covers on each side – which would make the advantages of spoked wheels even more tenuous since at that point the only substantive difference is a few hundred grams of weight. If you're riding unsupported, discs make no sense at all because, apart from the other issues, they're very hard to fix if you damage one.

Across both supported and unsupported, the tendency is towards electronic gears. Cable gears are simpler, don't need to be charged and are easier to fix, but they need more force to operate, and there will come a point in any ultra ride when that force becomes an issue. Even in 12-hour races back in the 2000s, by 10–11 hours the tendons in my wrists would start to complain about gear shifting, and I'd end up having to grip the bar-end lever with a full fist and a straight wrist like I was pulling a pint. Often as not

I'd leave the gear where it was and just wait for the road to come good again. I've had the same problem in even fairly short rides if the road surface is rough enough.

Still, I applaud everyone who still uses mechanical gears. At an aesthetic level I like the idea that you don't need to plug your bike into a socket to make it work properly. It means you're crossing a continent using nothing but your own effort. Yes, I'm aware this makes me a Luddite. And yes, I'm aware that the fact I wouldn't do it myself also makes me a hypocrite.

Similarly, hydraulic disc brakes have taken over from rim brakes in all except a small minority of cases. Partly that's just because that's what a modern top-end bike is built for and a cable just won't go round the required bends. But the biggest plus is it lets you run wider wheel rims and consequently wider tyres – for asphalt events, 30 mm and up, more for events with a lot of off-road elements. That's a win all round, because they'll be both more comfortable and, certainly at the speeds you ride an ultra, they'll be faster because there's less rolling resistance.

There's another advantage for an unsupported rider: disc brake set ups are more forgiving of a wheel that's gone out of true or been damaged than rim brakes. As long as the tyre will go through the frame, you're fine. That's a lot of latitude for a poppadum-shaped wheel compared to the few millimetres of latitude you have with rim brakes.

The downside is that while hydraulic brakes are a very reliable component, if they do go wrong it's properly difficult to fix. It's almost certainly a bike-shop job. About the best you can do in the meantime is use the other brake and hope it doesn't develop an issue, which isn't a reassuring mindset for taking on an Alpine descent. If you do need to get something fixed mid-race, you'd find that, for instance, it's easier to find spares for a Shimano set up than a SRAM set up.

There is, of course, also the question of what spares you take with you on an unsupported race. You can carry half a bike shop around for a fortnight, and never need it. You can take nothing and find a trivial problem derails your whole race. (Interesting bit of history – in 1937, Charles Holland, the first UK rider to survive for longer than a day of the Tour de France, had his race finished off just a few stages before Paris when his bike pump broke. He was riding in the independent, unsupported category, so there was no one to help him, and that was that.)

It's a weight:benefit analysis. I've broken just two chains in my whole cycling life, one because it was ancient, one because it was from a duff batch, and neither because of any inherent chain-snapping prowess on my part. I would still take some spare chain links if I was on a long ride because they weigh 2.5 g each and the only other way to fix a broken chain is to tie it together with a cable tie, make sure the repair is on the bottom run of chain, and shuffle the pedals backwards and forwards to keep it there but nudge the sprockets round. And that's no way to go anywhere. In the same period I've destroyed probably 40 tyres, and they are if anything more difficult to fake. All the same, I would not take one of those because they weigh a hundred times as much as the chain links.

The classic pre-race coverage of the TCR does not consist of asking the racers about their training, their hopes and expectations or even their inspiration. It consists of asking what's in their luggage. It's like sports journalism conducted by a customs official.

There's a fair consensus on bags – a frame bag, a bar bag, a top tube bag and a saddle pack. The saddle pack sometimes sits on a lightweight rack, to get the weight a bit lower and stop any swaying. Some riders drop the bar bag because of its poor aerodynamics, and/or its effect on the bike's handling. Most set ups end up somewhere between 8 and 15 litres of volume.

A big first sort out is where riders are planning to sleep. If you're intending to find hotels, you don't need a bulky sleeping bag or a bivvy bag or a mat. A few riders even wait till the weather forecast before deciding whether to go equipped for rough-ish sleeping.

Down jackets are a standard item – you can ride in them, sleep in them, put them on if you're stuck in a queue at a border crossing. Bike shoes are often supplemented with a pair of flip-flops for running into shops or coffee stops. Also, for running into a shop, a lot of riders take a musette or something similar so that firstly they're not carrying their shopping in their arms and secondly so they can jump back on the bike and unpack and stow as they ride.

A lightweight lock is a normal precaution for food stops. Though one rider I interviewed about kit said, 'Yup, I always take a lock. And for the first few days I am always sure to lock the bike. By about five days in I stop locking it, and by a week in I spend most of the time I'm in the shop hoping that by the time I get back outside someone will have stolen the fucking bike and I can go home with my head held high.'

A PERFECT EQUILIBRIUM OF DISCOMFORT

Most riders use a single set of kit, and either ignore its gradual deterioration into a biohazard, or wash it at hotel stops and put it back on at whatever state of dryness it might or might not have reached. There's still a lot of bike clothing in the bags, because riders change mode for day and night, hot and cold, wet and dry and all combinations by adding or subtracting clothing like they're in a 3,000-km dressing-up game. Arm warmers, leg warmers, knee warmers, winter jerseys, hats, base layers, gloves, glove liners, oversocks, buffs, rain jackets. Depending on the route and local bylaws there might be a hi-viz vest in there. And there will always be a 'special' item – a scarf, a neck towel, a bandana – that a given rider insists has some unique utility. It amuses me that Christoph Strasser's list always includes swimming shorts – and he does, he told me, not infrequently stop for a swim.

Other than chain links, you might want zip ties, plugs for repairing tubeless tyres, spare inner tubes, tyre levers, and a pump and/or CO_2 inflator. If you're more paranoid, you'll take spare brake pads, shoe cleats, and perhaps even some spare spokes. You'll need chain lube, since that needs to go on every 200–300 km.

And you need sun cream, a toothbrush. You definitely need some wet wipes, since that's the closest brush with hygiene some riders have for days on end. Plasters, painkillers. Passport and credit cards. Eye mask and earplugs – a necessity if you want to sleep under a hedge and ignore the angry wildlife and the local coppers trying to wake you up, or get any meaningful rest at a truck stop hotel.

There's very little consensus on food and drink. Some riders take quite substantial quantities of carb drink mix, gels and electrolyte tablets. Some work on the basis that since they're never going to carry it all, they'll start as they'll have to finish and find what they need as they go.

This is a lot of stuff. You can edit ruthlessly – do you need an extra base layer if you take arm warmers and put them on below your jersey or down jacket? Can you use a buff as an eye mask without squishing your eyeballs? Are there things you can just leave out and hope for the best? Maybe you can ditch the tyre levers and hope that after a week on a bike you still have enough strength in your thumbs to hoick a tyre off a rim with your bare hands. You could ditch the inner tubes as well, and rely on a puncture repair kit. All of these are trade-offs in probability multiplied by time. It's interesting that there's no especially strong correlation between packing and final race result. Within reason, there seems to be an extent to which it's self-correcting.

Here are some things no one riding a long bike race worried about in the 1980s – USB-C, micro-USB, weird proprietary connectors, adaptors, power banks, buffer batteries or the bizarre sockets they have in Switzerland. Keeping things charged and working has become part of the challenge. When Michael Broadwith did the TCR he said one of the best moments was finding a cashier at an all-night gas station who would let him sleep on her floor behind the counter, and (at least as thrilling) let him plug in everything so that when he left every battery indicator he had was at 100%.

On the other hand, Shu Pillinger's TCR failure in 2017 was the result of a lot of different issues, but she said the last straw was that her electronics stopped charging. 'The race was in a heatwave, I was desperately dehydrated in the middle of Austria and nothing was charging off the dynamo. I was trying to ride at night and sleep in the heat of the day, but you need more electricity at night because of lights, and the backlight on my GPS. I had a tracker, so other people knew where I was, but I'd no phone and no GPS, so I didn't know where I was. If something went wrong, in this heatwave, I couldn't tell anyone about it, I couldn't call for help if I needed it. It was all a bit overwhelming. And I realized it wasn't fun anymore.'

You will need to power your phone, your GPS, your tracker and your lights. You might want to power a pair of earbuds, and you might take an MP3 player since they use battery more slowly than your phone for audio. It's not the glory days of the early Tours de France any longer.

The big divide is between those who take a couple of large power banks and rely on charging them and everything else when they stop, and those who run a dynamo. The power banks are simpler, but limiting. The dynamo is less restrictive, but a hassle to set up. It also adds a certain amount of drag – maybe 5 or 6 watts when you're going slowly, and up to 15 watts at higher speeds (30 kph, say). If you're riding at maybe only 100–200 watts, that's not totally trivial. The set up can be complicated. If you won't always be going fast enough to generate the sort of charging wattage needed, you'll need to charge a battery or power bank and then charge your devices from that, which reduces the efficiency. In practice there will always be something plugged in and, like Shu Pillinger, you'll always be hoping it doesn't mysteriously stop working. Fixing a puncture in the dark by a roadside is one thing. Electronic engineering is another.

One of the most significant kit differences between normal and ultra riding is lights. Most bike riders need lights only for an hour or two for rides finishing at dusk, or a commute, and often as not on roads that have street lights. Ultra lights have to be different. You're looking for horsepower because usually the roads you're on are very dark indeed, and you need battery life because you're probably riding from dusk till dawn.

In terms of sheer functionality, bike lights have seen more change in the last couple of decades than almost any other component. I have no idea how anyone used to set about riding a 24-hour time trial with an old pair of battery lights, but they did. Original accounts of 24-hour races regularly include riders who simply rode off the road and ended up in a hedge, or got felled by a kerb in the dark. If they had potholes in the 1950s like we have potholes in the 2020s, there would be riders who would still be missing today.

The 24-hour courses of old were more difficult as well – modern courses include multiple laps and circuits. The Mersey Roads course covers one of its laps something like 15 times, with the first few times in daylight, so you have a chance to learn it. For most of the twentieth century there were much more restrictive limits in the rules about how often any particular stretch of road could be used, so 24-hour races used to rove far and wide. In the 1960s, the North Road CC 24-hour used to start near Stansted Airport in Essex and reached as far as Ely in Cambridgeshire, a more than 80-mile round trip. Riders were on unfamiliar roads, in the dark, relying on a 20 watt bulb if they were lucky.

Go back a bit further and they were using oil lamps. If you want to know how much light escapes from an oil lamp, it's worth knowing that at organized feed stops they used to position someone up the road to shout when a rider was approaching because you could shout further than the light could shine. I have absolutely no idea how anyone stayed on the road. I'd say I don't know how they didn't get hopelessly lost, but in fact they regularly did. One account from the time, written by a rider, mentions that his wife spent five hours driving around East Anglia trying to find him as he hurtled through the darkness somewhere he was never supposed to be, like Bury St Edmunds. And distance covered off course doesn't count.

For the first 24-hour I rode, I used two lights with a combined output of around 600 lumens, compared to less than 200 lumens for a 20 watt filament bulb (and you'd need a much, much bigger battery for the filament bulb). For the second race I upgraded to a single light made by the West Sussex-based company Exposure Lights that was a bit brighter than the previous two, but which also had an accelerometer that detected my speed and roughness of road surface, so it got brighter when I was going faster or riding a rougher bit of road. It worked brilliantly.

You can run brighter lights – if you run it flat out, the one I used in my second 24-hour will reach 3,200 lumens on fast sections – but the limit is battery life. Most of the lights are designed for two to three hours of use, and while they're a much smaller package than the old systems (the battery for which was so large it needed to be placed in a bottle cage with wires up to the light), they're still not tiny, something like the size of a mini-can of Coke. If you wanted to run a modern light at its brightest setting for the hours of darkness, you'd need to take an extra battery pack with you or swap lights.

The worst thing in the dark is potholes, which arrive so fast that you barely dare glance down at a computer, and stretches of road that don't have a white line or a clear edge of some sort. On the Mersey Roads course there is a stretch of several miles on the night circuit that doesn't have a white line, but rather a high kerb that blends into the colour of the road surface, a narrow footpath that's the same colour as the kerb, and a wall. It was very easy to imagine drifting left in the dark and the torrential rain, hitting the kerb, surfing across the footpath and braining myself on the wall. (Although there were points where I thought, 'Would that really be so bad?') Some 24-hour events are even harder on lights – the 24-hour 'World Championships' in the Californian desert east of San Diego happens in November, when it's dark for more than 13 hours. (Although the roads are pretty straight, and there's not a whole heap to hit.)

For multi-day races, the considerations depend very much on supported versus unsupported. On a supported race, you can keep your lights charged. But, more to the point, on most supported races the regulations require your support car to be behind you at night, with its lovely headlights. Once you get used to the slightly creepy shadows, it takes a lot of the stress off. You can happily sit further out into the road, and someone can yell at you if you start to drift off course.

Unsupported racers who don't use dynamos are, of course, in a world of trying to get lights charged, and balance battery life against the next charging opportunity to decide how much vision they're going to allow themselves at any given moment.

Long distance riders end up with a much more intimate relationship with their bikes than short distance racers. For a start, they almost certainly own their own stuff, rather than have it provided by a team. They pick and trial components, they devise mash ups of different companies' products. They worry about it all for months before a race.

It's personal in another way. You're out there for a long time, and the bike is the only real constant in life. A lot of ultra riders talk to their bikes – though they don't always admit it. They give them names, they make very individual modifications. Unlike the Tour de France or the Olympics, every bike that gets lined up at the start of RAAM, TCR or a 24-hour race will be different. And it matters. It's not just aerodynamics, as is almost the case for other events. It's a complicated mix of comfort, weight, durability. And it's one of the pleasures of ultra racing.

9

A 3 a.m. Lesson in Trust

In 1892, T.A. Edge of the Anfield Bicycle Club attacked the Land's End to John O'Groats record. The organizer for the attempt was John Davenport Siddeley, whose capacity for getting stuff done still stands as a beacon today.

Records in that era were paced. For every mile of the ride, the recordman would be accompanied by and sheltered by at least one, usually two, other riders. They'd ride for maybe 50 miles before being replaced by some fresh pacers. The rest of bike racing was the same – almost all road and track events in the UK were paced. On the track it was often by four-rider quads or five-rider quints, because that was the only way to go fast enough.

Siddeley's task, then, was to coordinate a schedule for the four-day ride. It had to account for the ferries needed in Scotland in an era when most firths were unbridged, because the ferries worked to a timetable and clearly no one wanted Edge to be left waiting. He established – by letter – which of the ferries would be prepared to wait upon receipt of a telegram telling them Edge was on his way and which wouldn't, then worked out where his rider needed to be and when. That allowed him to calculate when Edge needed to leave Land's End, more than two days before reaching the first crossing.

Then he had to arrange 17 or so pacing teams – between 30 and 40 riders, plus spares. These were usually the best riders from local clubs along the route. He had to tell them roughly what times they would be needed and the route they'd be responsible for guiding.

Then he sat down with a railway timetable and worked out how all these riders were getting to and from their start and finish points, because, of course, the only means of transport in 1892 were horses, walking, cycling and trains. Even then there were no direct trains from Cornwall to the North, and in Scotland there was only one train a day from Inverness to Wick. While he was at it, he worked out how he and the other helpers were getting from place to place to support Edge so that he had a friendly face and a spare bike every few miles along the route.

He followed that with finding suitable inns along the route through 74 villages and towns where Edge and all these other people could be fed, at all hours of the day and night, and ordering food.

And finally, as the attempt unfolded, as he dashed north via train and bicycle he dispatched telegram after telegram to alert inns, ferrymen, pacers and helpers as to expected arrival times and any assistance needed. He even ended up pacing Edge himself from Exeter to Taunton and from Wick to John O'Groats when other pacers failed to get there in time. Never mind the recordman, in the four days of the record Siddeley himself slept for less than six hours.

Edge did indeed set a new record. It lasted just a few weeks until another organizer laid on a similar effort that allowed L. Fletcher to take the record under four days for the first time. It probably involved a lot of the same pacers, innkeepers, ferrymen and telegram boys.

Siddeley himself went on to found car and aircraft manufacturing empires that still existed under his name into the 1970s, and eventually became the first Baron Kenilworth.

Organizing a paced record in the pre-car, pre-telephone era was probably something of a high-water mark. But even if we're past the sort of conditions that led an Edwardian End-to-Ender to bribe a Firth of Forth ferry captain to slow down and wait for a helper frantically trying to catch up in a rowing boat, the sheer logistical challenge of getting from one place to another is still considerable.

You can divide the issues pretty much down the middle into supported and unsupported events – while the physiology and psychology of all long events have a lot in common, exactly how you set about the event depends on whether you're alone.

If you want to do something like RAAM, you need people. You need vehicles and quite a lot of cash. For a solo RAAM rider, the general recommendation of the organizers is that you need eight crew and two vehicles. If you're not based in North America already, the estimates of how much it costs vary a bit, but the figure of $40,000 is quoted fairly regularly. So the first challenge a RAAM rider has is finding that amount of money, because if you don't do that, it doesn't matter how good a rider you are. Other events can be a little more affordable, not least because the entry fees are a bit lower, but none of it is cheap. Even for a shortish (500-mile) supported ultra race in Western Europe I looked at doing instead of taking up 24-hour time trialling, the sheer cost of the entry fees combined with the compulsory requirements for vehicles and signage stopped me dead, even before I'd started looking for a crew.

I sat in on some RAAM official seminars, which contained a lot of good advice and some terrifying stories of disasters. They had a lot of pictures of RVs upside down or in small pieces after tired, hurrying drivers drove them off the road. They had stories about crews falling out with each other, the rider falling out with the crew, and crews whose inadequacy effectively ended the race of a rider who, better looked after, might have done quite well. They even had a story about a rider whose support crew included both his wife and his girlfriend. His girlfriend knew about his wife. His wife did not know about his girlfriend. That got messy.

Psychologist Josephine Perry has worked not just with ultra riders, but with the rest of the crew. A supported race is, after all, a team effort. She made another point that I'd never really thought of: 'Being on a support crew is hard. They've got potentially a long time living together in a difficult environment, not sleeping, eating badly. They don't normally know each other, and none of them are in their usual routine, taking their normal exercise, things like that. Often support teams are made up of the sort of people who ride long events themselves, so they've got valuable experience. But it also means they're probably a bit stubborn,

A 3 A.M. LESSON IN TRUST

maybe a bit introverted. Maybe that's what you need to be a rider, but as a team member you might not be the most malleable person to sit beside in a car for a week. These people will piss each other off. On something like RAAM, the crew are at least as likely to go wrong as the rider.'

I repeated to her the story about the rider whose team had included both his wife and his girlfriend. 'He should probably have planned for that,' she said. 'Because I'd have to say that was pretty foreseeable.'

A friend who rode RAAM several years ago experienced problems with his crew. He'd employed a nutritionist as part of his team, because that's clearly a useful skill set to have behind you. His crew chief overruled everything the nutritionist suggested from the moment they rolled past the start, on the basis that he'd ridden the race before and experience outweighed expertise. He followed that up with a string of complaints about carrying a 'deadweight' person across a continent, on the basis that she wasn't now contributing anything. I have no idea who was right (and neither does the rider, really), but unless the nutritionist was amazingly laid-back, it seems likely to have created a certain amount of tension.

The one positive to that experience was that the rider didn't know anything about it at the time. But it's clearly a poorly set-up team – in that instance the rider said his mistake was creating a tight team that supported him during the build up with things like coaching, nutrition and psychology, then at the last minute dropping in a crew chief with several actual races behind him to be in charge at the event itself.

There is a very obvious problem at the heart of any crewed race. It's that it is the rider's project. They decide they want to do it, they put the finance in place, they find the crew. They deal with equipment sponsors, they source non-sponsor equipment. Often as not they book hotels and hire vehicles and buy the plane tickets. For months on end their whole lives are taken over with planning a huge adventure and whistling out of thin air what very quickly starts to feel like an army of people and a warehouse of stuff, accompanied by a boardroom of sponsors who all need some of your time.

(It is an aggravating truism that sponsors only want your time in the run up to an event. They don't want it afterwards, when you have all the time in the world, because if you don't win, or you don't finish, you're no longer any use to them. In the run up, everyone is a potential winner or at least a potential story, so their value to a sponsor is much greater.)

Riders have to do this while trying to train, usually for hours a day. They prepare psychologically. They experiment with nutrition. They do all the things in this book, all of which take time. More often than not they're also trying to hold down a day job in the face of increasing exasperation from their employer, who will be learning the hard way that the angels and demons that drive an ultra rider to do extraordinary things for themselves will not drive them to do extraordinary things for you.

And then, when the race arrives, they have to hand all of this time, money and commitment to someone else. Because you cannot, you absolutely cannot, manage

A 3 A.M. LESSON IN TRUST

the crew and the race from the bike. Even if, in the early stages, you can think about all of that as well as your own efforts, you won't by the mid-event. By the end there's a good chance you'll barely be a functioning human, never mind a competent manager. The trust between rider and crew needs to be total. It's nice if it goes both ways, but ultimately a rider needs to accept that the crew is now in charge, the crew will look after them, and the crew now knows best. There's a process of letting go that most riders find very difficult – as Josephine Perry said, most of them are single-minded, stubborn individuals, and to be honest most of them are control freaks, because that's how you get yourself to the start line.

The reason you have to trust your crew is just that you're an unreliable witness as well as an unreliable boss. In my second 24-hour, at about 2.30 a.m., I suddenly started to struggle. The night had become much colder than forecast, only 7 or 8 degrees, and I hadn't enough clothes on – just a base layer and a race suit. I didn't notice it getting colder because it happened gradually, and it was against my expectations from the forecast. It left me unsure of what the unpleasant sensation was. There was also an unwillingness to stop for more kit, and to then wear something unaerodynamic for several hours because of the distance it would lose me, so I had an element of denial going on as well.

I know what you're thinking – you're thinking, 'How can you be freezing cold and not know? How can you, a man obsessed with performance, not realize that hypothermia is even slower than a jersey that you haven't refined in a wind tunnel?' To which I say, 'Exactly.'

That gave way to gastrointestinal issues. I've mentioned this before, back when I was dealing with nutrition. But it's as much a story about my team as it is about my stomach. I started being sick, repeatedly, as I rode. The vomiting was almost explosive, as if everything I'd consumed in 12 hours was fighting to get out, and it took every scrap of energy I had with it. I remember thinking that I needed to try to do it facing backwards because of the sheer propulsive force of the jet.

I crept miserably back to the crew base, about 20 minutes' ride away, and stopped. 'That's it,' I said, as I stood there with vomit dripping picturesquely off me.

'Hmm,' said Mike and Chris, keeping a certain distance.

'I'm just empty, it's just fallen apart. I'm finished. I'm sorry, and thank you, but that's the end. I got that wrong.'

'OK,' said Mike. 'Come and sit in the van and warm up a bit.'

I sat in the van (Chris's van, so letting me into it was noble of her). They gave me an anti-sickness tablet and some plain water. It was nice and warm in the van, and I was completely reconciled to this being the end. I wasn't happy about it, but I was sure that I'd done my best off a very limited training run in, and if nothing else I'd definitively established that my new liquid-only nutrition strategy was not something to repeat. There was no way back from where I was. Sometimes people fail.

'Have a sleep,' said Mike. 'Take 15 minutes.'

So I went to sleep. It didn't seem like 15 minutes later that Mike woke me up. He later confirmed that it wasn't. It was about four. 'I just waited till it looked like you were asleep, then I woke you up,' he said.

A 3 A.M. LESSON IN TRUST

When Chris gave me the jelly snakes and told me I needed to get some glucose in, a horrible suspicion began to dawn on me that they weren't making a plan for me to go home.

They took me for a little walk that turned out to be back to the bike. 'OK,' said Mike. 'Just see what you can do. I'll come after you down the course in the van, and if you need to stop, just stop and I'll pick you up. But just try to get from layby to layby. Take it slowly.' He gave me the rest of the packet of sweets to put in a pocket, and literally dressed me into a warm top like you would a toddler. It was kind of humiliating.

Twenty minutes later I was racing again. I felt fine, back in an aero position, trying to hit the right power numbers. I'd lost too much time to get back on terms for any sort of a result, but I ended up in much better shape at the end of the race than I had the previous year – I was about 2 kph faster in the last hours of the race, and felt an awful lot better. I felt like I was still racing, rather than just waiting for it all to end.

It was great support work. The jelly snakes were good, but not as good as Mike and Chris. I hadn't ridden to them with plans to debate the issue, I'd ridden back to quit. The only reason I'd even ridden back to the team at all was that if I'd stopped on the course and called them to come and get me, the quitting would have taken longer. What was lucky was that trusting them was easy. Mike and Chris have each won several 24-hour events. So I had some faith in them, and I didn't ultimately think I knew better than them. I'd expected them to agree with me, and when they didn't, I was prepared to give their way a chance.

It helped that they weren't confrontational. No one told me not to be stupid, no one told me to get on with it. I was put back into the race very gently, so gently that there was almost nothing to fight against. It was made so clear that I could stop if I wanted to that it would have been oddly aggressive to even attempt to argue.

They were in a better position to see what was going on. I wasn't the first rider that night to succumb to the cold and its consequences. Mike and Chris had been through similar things, and they'd seen others go through similar things. I'd heard a lot of ultra riders talk about the way that things can always get better, and how critical it is never to lose your grip on that. I am amazed that there was a way back from where I was. In a way I felt better about the whole experience after the race when Chris said that, despite her role in getting me going again, she was actually a bit surprised that it had worked. 'Seeing you in full aero [position] on the finishing circuit made it worthwhile – I really didn't expect that,' she said. So even to an experienced onlooker, it had at least constituted a proper crisis, not a minor tantrum. For my own part I was surprised how passive and obedient I was. I did what I was told, like a lamb. On a long, supported race, there's the potential for repeated incidents like this – I'm sure if I took on RAAM they'd run at the rate of at least one a day. And if the rider doesn't trust the crew, and the crew isn't sympathetic to the rider, there are only so many of them they'll get through.

*

A 3 A.M. LESSON IN TRUST

The whole show gets exponentially more complicated when your supported race isn't running round a set of smallish circuits. For RAAM and similar events, as I've already mentioned, a solo rider typically needs eight people, running two vehicles. One of the vehicles stays close to the rider. In the early parts of the race, the rules usually prevent them following directly behind during the day; instead they have to leapfrog past the rider to provide support from the roadside. This leapfrogging will happen pretty regularly, because the idea is to keep the rider in sight all the time. They have to follow directly behind at night to protect them and provide a bit of illumination – most of the follow cars have a lot of lights on the front. In the later days, the car follows behind all the time. The switch is partly because of the deteriorating condition of the rider, and partly because the race has spread out a bit so the whole shebang is less in the way of everyone else.

Crewing the follow vehicle is a full-time job. The driver drives the van. The front seat passenger drives the cyclist. They've usually got a tablet and a route description, and probably a laptop for tracking other data including telemetry from the rider, nutrition notes, timings of reminders for the rider when to eat and drink – unless there's a third team member in the back seat doing that bit. They've got a radio or loudspeaker mic for hectoring.

(The official route description for RAAM is very detailed – it is many, many pages. Even so, it frequently has notes that underline the challenge – at one point it notes there are 'no distinguishable landmarks' for 120 miles. At another it observes there's nothing in most of a day's riding for the rider to look at or think about except riding. It reminded me of a support crew member who assured me that there are parts of Kansas where it's perfectly possible to see a bike light from a range of 8 miles. The route guide also contains slightly random historical notes, such as the fact that the town of Ulysses in Grant County, Kansas was named after Ulysses S. Grant. I suppose you can always read them to your rider if you've run out of porn.)

The follow vehicle (typically a minivan) also has spares – bikes and wheels, clothing, shoes, bits and pieces like aero bar parts, pedals, chains... anything breakable. There's a first aid kit, there's an awful lot of food. The other vehicle has more stuff, and options for sleeping and cooking. One of the debates is whether this vehicle is a full-fat RV or something smaller, like a Mercedes Sprinter, probably in combination with some motels. In an RV the size of an ocean liner you can sleep anyone who needs to sleep, cook anything you want to cook and carry any amount of stuff. On the other hand it's difficult to park, which has an impact on things like buying groceries quickly, and which also means it can't really fill in well for the following vehicle if there's a problem because you can't stop along the road.

RVs are also more expensive than other solutions, and even if you have the budget, you will have trouble renting one. For one thing, you'll almost certainly have to return it in California, so some lucky campers will get to spend several days post-race driving back the way they came. For another, RAAM teams do not have the most glittering reputation among the RV hire outfits in California. Most of them have the dates of the race on their calendar. They will ask a lot of questions if that's the rental period you want. Other, less high-profile races won't have that exact problem, but they'll have all the rest.

However well you plan things, the crew will have problems to deal with. Shu Pillinger's crew had a terminal follow vehicle breakdown, which they solved by getting her to have a sleep while they transferred everything (computers, spares, lights) to a different team car. It was late in the race. Shu says that when she woke up, 'I was puzzled about how or why the follow car had changed colour. That seemed odd. But I just accepted it. I didn't find out the reason till afterwards.' I like this vignette – it tells you something about the condition of a rider, the trust they have, and the acceptance of whatever is going on around them. Shu's description of a supported ultra rider as a 'toddler' fits perfectly.

As to what the crew does, they do everything except pedal. Food and drink, dealing with illness and injuries, navigation, and above all planning. Where to get groceries, where to get fuel, where to do some laundry (remember bike riders can get through huge amounts of kit). There are tactical elements. Faster outfits will try to coordinate their rider's sleep stops with the weather forecast to make sure they don't spend time asleep when they could have been using the best bit of tailwind. They'll try to have a better-rested rider for some of the difficult sections, like the climbs in the Rockies and the Appalachians, and work out where to swap to a climbing bike if that's part of the plan. They're all small details, but the race lasts a week. Ten minutes a day might be worth an hour and a half by the time you're finished.

I find all of this a fascinating challenge. It's a mix of riding, management, logistics and tactics. The outstanding problem with it is simply one of resources. People, money and time. Long, fully supported races have become a major undertaking, which is beyond the means of most 'normal' ultra riders. You need deep pockets, sponsorship, or to set it up as a charity ride. Even if you do that, you're realistically looking for a lot of volunteers to crew. The trend over the last few years to unsupported races is clear, and it's understandable. Even the doyen of RAAM, four-time winner Christoph Strasser, said that the main reason he'd entered the unsupported Transcontinental Race was because that sort of event was where the competition was getting more intense.

Unsupported racing is simpler and cheaper, obviously. Except that the rider has to manage everything. In turn that means a smaller proportion of the challenge is purely athletic. No one ever retired from RAAM because they weren't engineer enough to get their dynamo to work properly, but things just like that can happen in unsupported races. Whether you think that's a good thing or a bad thing is, of course, up to you. It's one reason that women and men compete on more of a level playing field as the distance goes up, and all the more so in unsupported events. Strength and raw aerobic ability matter less. Route planning, logistics, eating, managing sleeping, coping with the psychological demands of the race and dealing with problems are all things that do not offer either sex any clear advantage. They're down to the individual.

The non-pedalling challenges of unsupported racing start a long way back. You frequently have to plan your own route from start to finish, probably including some checkpoints and maybe some compulsory sections of route, either for safety, or for added challenge. Or, as one or two riders complained about gravel parcours on the Transcontinental Race, 'Because the organizers thought we weren't getting enough punctures as it was.'

The variations in route are an essential element in the dot-watching experience. It's probably the most fascinating aspect of following an event – when the field splits, sometimes separated by many kilometres, or when one or two of the leading riders suddenly do something entirely unexpected. There's often a day or two waiting to see if it's going to come good when the riders come back together. In the 2024 TCR race, Christoph Strasser turned round and rode the 'wrong way' back up a parcours he'd already completed, because he reckoned the route he could access that way was easier for the next section of the race. It was an original idea, even if it didn't make a revolutionary difference to the results. And it meant an entire community of dot-watchers could be very confused for a few hours till a social media update told us what he was up to.

TCR rider James Hayden reckoned route planning could occupy as much as 100 hours of his time. 'It might well be a better use of time to sit down and do some routing than to go out training,' he told me. He breaks the route into stages, usually between checkpoints, and then starts by using a GPS route planner. Then he refines it through a series of iterations – maybe he looks at a shorter route with more climbing, or maybe the other way around. You might also use a longer route that avoids a large town, or follows a river, because that will be fairly flat. Towns can be double-edged – it's slower riding, but it's an easy place to buy food. And riding through a town early in the morning or at night is a different thing from doing it at nine o'clock in the morning in terms of speed.

There are other subtleties. 'I also look at the likely weather, especially the wind direction, and try to find a route that takes as much advantage of that as I can,' he says. 'Sometimes I save two different routes on my bike computer, and pick which one will work best with whatever the weather is when I get there.'

*

Riders also use the input you can get from Street View, which will tell you about the size of a road and potentially the quality of the surface. You can contact local riders, and get their advice. You can look at a Strava heatmap – it will show you the roads that are nicer to ride, if everything else is equal. You need to look at the facilities en route – even in Western Europe there are areas where if you picked the wrong route on the wrong day or the wrong time of day you might struggle to find an open shop.

There are sometimes problems that you can't avoid. Border posts, especially in Europe, are often at the tops of hills that it might have been nice to bypass. And they're also frequently on major highways. Major highways have another problem, which is that they are often the most direct way to get to places, but also the absolute worst place to ride a bike. On a record ride around Australia, World Tour pro Lachlan Morton frequently had to simply ride off the road to get out of the way of truck drivers who could see him, but just didn't care. And Ian Walker told me that on his trans-Europe record he spent several hours on a major Polish highway that was, practically speaking, the only way to get to where he was going, but which was nose to tail trucks the whole way. 'It was just frightening,' he said. 'I didn't have much choice, but it was a terrible place to end up riding a bike.'

Although of course, trucks do come with a side benefit – they move air in the direction you want to go, so you might be terrified, but you are at least going slightly faster. It makes more difference the faster you go. In 24-hour time trialling, many riders preferred a different iteration of the championship course to the ones I raced on, a version that included a road with significant lorry traffic that ran all night.

There are some limits to your route planning. Christoph Strasser told me he went to recce some parcours in Romania for a Transcontinental, not all that far from his home in Austria. 'Some people felt that wasn't quite in the spirit of the event,' he says. 'That everyone should race under the same conditions, and that not everyone has the time and money, or opportunity, to go and look in advance. And maybe they're right.' There are similar (mild) criticisms of riders with sponsors, who have the option of better equipment and potentially more time to train.

(As a former pro rider in a different part of cycling I'd add that sponsors don't come free – there are obligations. And you only attract them once you've already achieved a certain amount off the back of your own overdraft. But I'd accept that sponsorship, even short of professional status, starts to blur the lines on a cycling discipline that is still essentially amateur in its ethos.)

Along with the actual route, there are other details. You can save every gas station and supermarket on your chosen route as a waypoint on your GPS, so you know how far away the next one is. While you can't book a hotel in advance, you can make sure you've saved the location of all the ones that have a 24-hour check-in. Same with suitable bike shops and pharmacies. It saves you from having to start looking for things in an emergency.

You can go further. Fiona Kolbinger pointed out to me that every Aldi or Lidl supermarket is laid out the same way: 'Bakery first, then sweets, then fruit. It means you don't stand around pondering. You go in, you shop, you leave.' She is not the only unsupported ultra rider to make exactly this observation. There is another benefit. Not only is the layout the same, much of the food is the same. In general riders know nutritionally what they're looking for, but you can still waste a lot of time standing there deciphering the nutritional information on unfamiliar packaging, possibly in an unfamiliar language. Buying 10,000 kcal isn't an easy or quick job, and if the options are all the same each time, you can be back outside a little sooner.

A different way to solve the problem is to rely on gas stations. There are more of them, they're on all the major routes and don't demand you go into a town to find them, and best of all they have a very small selection so there's practically no dithering to be done even if you want to. You

A 3 A.M. LESSON IN TRUST

can be in and out very fast indeed, if you're not too fussy about what you emerge with. Given the preponderance of sweets and other carb-heavy 'junk' in most riders' diets, it can work perfectly well for at least some of the food stops. As an added bonus you can probably see your bike for the entire time you're in there.

After food in order of obsession comes sleeping. There are really only two ways to do this – you sleep in a hotel (or hostel or similar), or you sleep somewhere by the road. Hotels are slower; by the time you've checked in and found your room (and maybe had to find somewhere else to keep your bike) and explained to an incredulous receptionist that you won't need breakfast because while you appreciate it's midnight and you look like you've been travelling since they invented the bicycle, you'll be leaving again in four hours.

On the other hand, you can wash yourself and your kit, you can charge every electronic device you own, and you probably get a better sleep. If you sleep in a hotel every night, you can potentially carry a bit less kit, like a sleeping bag.

Sleeping rough is faster and cheaper and somewhat in the spirit of the discipline. It can be a magical experience if you wake up somewhere amazing as the dawn breaks. Or it can go wrong. Sometimes riders pick a bad spot. In 2022, back to TCR as defending champion after the Covid pandemic, Fiona Kolbinger stopped for a sleep in Žatec in Czechia, and ended up getting robbed as she slept in a skatepark.

'It was a stupid place to sleep,' she says. 'I was being stubborn. I'd decided on the route, and I'd decided I was going to go through this town. And then it was time to have a sleep, and I saw this skatepark and thought it looked fine. I was lazy – I should have looked for a better spot, but I didn't. While I was asleep, someone took my credit cards, my ID card and the other stuff from my purse, and my race tracker. I was lucky that I was using the alarm on my phone, so it was right by my head and they didn't get that. They didn't take my passport, which I'd kept with me when I went to sleep. So in a way I was lucky. I had my phone, so I could cancel all the cards, and I had my passport, which meant I could get across borders. I quickly realized I had everything I needed to keep going in the race.'

And she kept going. When she told me about it, I said that at the very least I'd have lost half a day over it. Just the shock of it, the problems it was going to produce. 'But that wouldn't have helped,' was her reply. 'I could have gone home – I wasn't actually all that far away from home, I could have ridden there in a few hours. But then what? Sit around at home doing all the paperwork for the Czechia police? That was not how I was going to spend my holiday time. I thought to myself, "There's no justification for scratching from the race because of this. There's no reason I can't continue." So I continued.'

She had to track her own route to the next checkpoint before she could get a new race tracker. And she had to deal with the police reports and follow up while she was on the move. But she continued. She made going on with the race sound like the most natural thing she could have done. I think most of us would have been a great deal more rattled by the experience.

A 3 A.M. LESSON IN TRUST

There have been doubts raised about the wisdom of public tracking – it means anyone, anywhere can see where any of the riders are at any time, and especially see when they stop to sleep. But the tracking dots are also almost the entire race as far as any fans are concerned. You shouldn't underestimate the excitement of logging on to a website each morning to see where everyone has got to overnight, then flicking back every hour or two all day to watch a race creep almost imperceptibly across your screen. Losing or reducing the coverage would be a blow to the whole concept of the races.

In a strange way, Kolbinger's experience stands out. It's amazing how small a role problems, crises and full-blown disasters play in unsupported racing. Ultra riders seem to have an extraordinary level of resilience. It's not unusual to hear someone say they had a trouble-free race, other than the bit where they had to walk 11 miles down a gravel parcours because they destroyed both their tyres. Partly it's the spirit of the thing, partly it's just the sheer distances and time involved that allow events to sink into the details, but it's genuinely astonishing how relaxed riders are about most things. Coming from a background in shorter distance racing, I have a tendency to assume that for a good race, everything must work perfectly and the only real variable will be how well I execute a race plan. Nothing will break, I won't get a puncture at a critical moment, and if I do, that's the end of it all.

As the distances go up things that I instinctively want to classify as issues, problems, crises and disasters tend to just become part of the race. Sure, you need the legs and the stomach and the belief that things will always get better. But you also need to be able to fix a puncture in the dark and the rain, repair a chain using two stones, or find a bike shop to bleed your brakes at seven o'clock on a Sunday morning. Dealing with this stuff is part of what the good riders are good at.

Only occasionally do you get a straightforward mistake or accident that just wrecks everything. In the Transcontinental in 2024, the relatively unknown 22-year-old Victor Bosoni was running with the leaders, when 48 hours into the race he realized he'd left his wallet and passport at a gas station 270 km behind him. He had to go back and get it, a ride that involved going back over the Grossglockner and Brenner passes. He rejoined the race, but it was an abrupt end to being a contender.

In practice the things that really do stop people tend not to be mechanical or logistical – you can fix those, even if it's not easy and it takes time. It's usually the rider. And it's always the unexpected. Shu Pillinger said she'd never in her life suffered from saddle sores until she started tipping water over herself on a very hot stretch of race. The water ran down her back into her shorts, and started to cause sores. It's the classic example of a problem you didn't see coming. Who would ever have checked for that in training?

The best riders are good at a sort of constant status update. 'Do I need to eat? Do I need to drink? Do I need sunscreen? When is the next chance to buy food, when is the chance after that, how much do I need and how soon? Where is the route going next – is there a climb coming? Or a descent where I might want to put a jacket on?' Even more dramatic decisions. 'Do I need to walk up this steep hill? Do I need to walk over this part of parcours to avoid punctures?' Long races aren't about pacing in the same way short races are, they're about keeping moving, about an instinct for the most time-efficient way to do things, about looking after yourself and not forgetting things.

In my old short distance world, the psychology always looked at the difference between an outcome goal and a process goal. An outcome goal was a result – I want to win. The thing is, wanting to win isn't much actual help. A process goal was one of the bits of behaviour that got you there, like keeping an aero position, riding at the right pace, eating and drinking. These are things that do help. In a short race, the pressure usually throws you onto the outcome goals and the challenge is to actually work through the process goals. For some long distance competitors, it seems almost the other way round. For days on end you have process goals to deal with – just getting through the days in one piece – and if you don't keep on top of them it's obvious that you're not going to get the result.

10

The Hutch Moment

If you arrive in the world of long distance racing from where I started, in short distance events, it's easy to assume that the main difference between them is just a matter of duration. I'll take the risk of sounding like an idiot and put that another way. Before I rode my first long event, I thought it was the same as a short event, just longer.

I expected the majority of issues to be the same, just at different points of the graph. So the physiology was the same, the biomechanics, the aerodynamics, all the rest of it. The difference would be that as you moved to the right along an x-axis of time, you'd settle on a different spot on the y-axis of the other thing. The only real change would be that you'd factor in a few things like comfort and the sustainability of a riding position, and the logistics of a crew or the practicalities of looking out for yourself. That model was how I initially concluded I would be very bad at it, then later concluded I might be quite good, before going toe-to-toe with reality and discovering the truth was in between those two.

What makes ultra racing more difficult than I'd initially assumed is that everything is interconnected, and to a significantly greater degree than for shorter distance rides. In short distance racing you can, to a large extent, look at elements like physiology, psychology and nutrition as three separate, if related items. To do well you certainly need to understand how they affect each other, but it's plausible for at least your first pass to examine them as different things. In ultra racing it's not so much that they're more closely related as that they're verging on being part of the same thing. You can't look at one of them without thinking about how it affects the others. And, of course, there are a few new elements in the equation as well.

In a short distance time trial, the key metric is simply how fast you can go. In a pro road race, it's how fast you can go in the finale. All the elements, plus maybe some tactics, feed into that, but the main objective remains fairly simple, and the vast majority of your problem is simply moving oxygen. That's why at that end of things aerobic capacity is what delineates a top performer. In long distance racing, speed is only part of it. There's how long you can last without sleep. How you recover from a bad spell. How well you can eat – but of course the state of your gut depends on how hard you're riding, and how hard you're riding depends on the nutrition up to that point. All of that depends on good decision making and durable psychology, which in turn depends more than anything else on how tired you are, which takes us back round to how long you can last without sleep. It's a gigantic flow chart comprised of almost nothing other than feedback loops. I tried to map out this notional flow chart, and it looked like I'd lifted it from a *New Scientist* cartoon.

This complexity is one of the reasons that successful ultra riders don't conform to the same basic template as each other. Another reason is that, unlike at the shorter distances, there are a lot of ways to be good at distance. One of the things I relished most as I did interviews for this book was the contrast in approach between Christoph Strasser and Fiona Kolbinger. Strasser is an athlete who works in a way that feels familiar from my own competitive history. For him, ultra racing was a little like I initially imagined it to be – short distance, but longer. Kolbinger is different, someone who doesn't train in any way I really understand, and whose competitive motivations are mixed with elements of adventuring and challenge. Strasser has strengths that include an aerobic ability that means he performs perfectly well on a short distance time trial. Kolbinger's strengths bend more towards resilience, focus and her ability to eat, absorb and burn anything that's not made of metal. It's two ways of achieving the same thing, and there's no way in which one is better than the other because in the end there's a simple way of assessing the balance of talents and the approach of the rider – the result.

This is also why women perform so well at ultra races. Men have some raw physical advantages that fizzle away as all the other elements of the game get more important, and as managing the relationships between them becomes more involved. As Fiona Kolbinger pointed out, neither gender has an advantage in eating or hydration, in aerodynamics, picking the right equipment, dealing with sleep deprivation, planning a route, or in finding the right place to buy food or booking a hotel that isn't hosting an all-night disco.

The interconnectedness leads directly to the next thing that you can't ignore about ultra racing – the psychology of it. First, there is the currently rather mysterious role that psychology plays in setting the limits of endurance physiology. But second, and more relevant here, most of the things you need to deal with are conscious decisions. In my old life, psychology was something that was rather front loaded – you spent a lot of time looking at things that happened before the race. How you cope with training, for example, by learning to work through hard sessions by finding the right motivational cues, whether it be literally thinking about glorious victory, or (more likely) finding the intermediate goals that you can use to work from week to week and month to month. Not totally unlike a training version of promising yourself you'll ride to the next junction, then have another look at where you're going next.

Then you'd look at pre-event arousal – controlling your nerves. So, a lot of relaxation exercises, a lot of analysing what you expected during the event to reduce the generalized fear of the unknown that keeps you awake for four nights before the race. Then you'd move onto thinking about the race itself, and visualizing all the scenarios that were likely to play out and how you'd respond if they did. You'd move on to rehearsing in your mind how you would execute each skill. I once spent a month visualizing each day how you make a start from an automatic timing gate for

THE HUTCH MOMENT

a track pursuit – an action covering a few tenths of a second that could gain you as much as a couple of bike lengths (it's not a lot, but it's only a four-minute race) if you got it right.

The whole purpose of that sort of thing is to make the race itself almost an autopilot experience. You are calm because you know what is likely to happen, you know how to respond to events almost without thinking and ideally you've done the right thing almost without a conscious decision. Even if something really unexpected happens, you've got more processing power left over to deal with it. Clearly that's an ideal, and different races will work out differently. But if you tried that sort of exhaustive mental preparation for an ultra race, after 15 years of visualizing different scenarios you'd have forgotten what you were doing it for.

To put it simply, in a short race perhaps 80% of the psychological discipline happens before you start the race and 20% happens during. In a long race, it might be close to the other way round. In a short race, the amount of mental effort you put into 'not just giving up and going home' is zero. In a long race, there will be long stretches of your time when you have to deal with that urge and neutralize it every minute or two. You need to prepare for it beforehand, by working out your motivation and doing some visualization, or working your way through a sort of flow chart so you know the implications of every action. Even just picking a slogan/mantra ('The best you can be right now', for example) can work brilliantly. But applying this preparation isn't a split-second thing. You can be deep in your own psychology for hours at a time.

There are decisions to be made, and they're not all that easy to prepare for, just because there are so many more moving parts. You can work them out for yourself – a shop is shut when it should have been open, a road that looked great on Street View is in reality almost unrideable, there's a tailwind you don't want to miss out on, or you're repeatedly sick and have to try to work out what you might be able to eat when the thought of anything at all makes you feel like curling up on the roadside and surrendering. On their own, one at a time, they're not completely unforeseeable. It's just that there are so many of them. They can come at you so fast. And you're already going to be exhausted and sleep deprived every time one of them appears.

There's the lack of rehearsal – it takes years to become an experienced ultra rider. I'd probably seen 90% of the things that could possibly happen in a 20-minute race by my second racing season. A lifetime wouldn't be long enough to see 90% of what can happen in ultra races. That's why ultra riders are so entertaining – even the most athletically focused of them is still an adventurer and a problem solver. What you need is not so much the experience of all the different things, it's the experience to accept that anything can happen and the temperament to deal with it or at least put up with it until it goes away. (Incidentally, one of the things I saw in my first two seasons was a race direction sign exploding as I passed it when it was struck by lightning. As far as I know I'm the only rider who has ever seen this.)

That's also why I think there's more luck involved in making yourself into a successful ultra rider. If you have the fortune to get it right, or at least right-ish, first time out it will be a huge help. If my first 12-hour had been like my third 12-hour, if I'd managed to find the coaching and science support that I only pulled together as my career went on, I'd probably have ridden a 24-hour 20 years before I did, and for all I know gone on to a glorious long distance career.

All of this means that it would be almost impossible to be so physically talented that your psychology didn't matter. You can contrast that with shorter events where the opposite is true – 'normal' sport is full of physical specimens so superb that almost nothing short of a full breakdown would stop them. I've run into several of them in my time, and despite what might be a deeply chaotic approach to being an athlete it's still hard not to be impressed.

That's not to say that physiology doesn't matter – it does. What's surprising, to me at least, is that the ideal physiology for ultra riding is not as different from other racing as you might expect. I'd always reckoned that in a time trial, if I could beat you over 10 miles I could beat you over 100, but that a 12-hour was totally different. In truth I think it's only different because of everything else. Pure physiology, in terms of aerobic ability and your ability to turn oxygen and sugar into movement, stays pretty much the same. So, to a large extent, does the way you'd train. I hadn't expected to prepare for a 24-hour race with short interval sessions and heat acclimatization, but I accepted very gratefully the idea that I wasn't going to be off to do a lot of seven-hour training rides.

And it's not to say that aerodynamics doesn't matter, or that equipment choices don't matter. It's just that the relationships are not the same, and none of them is a decision that you take and forget. You need to understand every compromise you've decided on because at some point you'll have to work it out again after something changes. If you have a sore back that means you can't reach the aero bars, or a damaged tyre that means you need to run an inner tube rather than tubeless, you need to know how that's going to affect everything else.

Ultra racing asks for a huge amount of responsibility from you as an individual. Even if you have a crew in a supported race, and even if you've managed to trust them to manage you and manage the race, the only person who is inside your head is you, and inside your head is where so much of this happens. I struggled to communicate effectively with my team in the races I did – when things got hard I just went quiet. I could have asked them to do anything within reason and they'd have done it, but I wasn't good enough at working out what were the very basic things I needed. Once I didn't eat for three hours because I couldn't think of anything we had in the coolers that I could face. Eventually they took to offering me a whole buffet – I'd get to where the team was based and there would be five people (some borrowed from other teams) lined out along 100 metres of road waving different things at me. Only at that point could I work out that what I wanted were some sour-flavoured energy chews. But I was terrible at helping them to help me the first time and only slightly better the second. With experience might come the ability to better see myself, where I was and what was happening to me. Or, of course, it might not.

In spite of my own inadequacies, I love the experience of the long races, and the company of the people that ride them. A very long time ago, after the one success of my early 12-hours, I told a reporter that I'd love to ride a 24-hour one day, and told him it was not because I thought I'd be particularly good at it, but because I thought there'd be things about the experience that I'd like. I was right about that.

For a start, while my rides have been a long way short of the best rides over a day, I'm still impressed at having ridden 486 miles. If I draw a circle of that radius on a map, it stretches from my home in Cambridge to Orkney to the north, Lyon to the south, most of the way to Berlin to the east and nowhere in particular in the North Atlantic to the west. On a simple, human-powered machine from the middle of the nineteenth century.

My focus on cycling for a whole career was about speed over short and middle distances. But perhaps the truth is that what bikes are best at is distance. There is something inspiring about the efficiency. When Fiona Kolbinger told me about how much of her motivation came from the idea of riding from the plains to the mountains, then to a different country, and how she loved to watch the landscape change as she rolled it past her with nothing but her own effort, it was something I'd never really contemplated before. I'd spent most of a lifetime doing training rides of a few hours, out and back, riding endlessly to nowhere and seeing the same roads day in and day out. Once, when someone with a firm grasp of the wrong end of the stick asked me how far I rode in a week and then worked out the savings in carbon emissions, I had to tell him that it would only have counted if I'd been planning to go and do my interval session in the car instead. To turn round now and think about how far you can go, with so little fuss and so little impact on anything around you, has been new.

It's also been a connection to a lot of other cyclists. For a start, it's been a direct line into cycling history. A nineteenth-century rider was proud of how far they could go first and how swiftly they could get there only second. In a world where the railways had only recently made the stagecoach obsolete, and where a horse was an expensive luxury, the idea of an ordinary person being able to travel independently by any means other than walking was novel. The idea of doing it at 12 mph, perhaps even more, for hours on end was revolutionary.

It goes straight back to the early road races as well. The object there was almost exactly the same as a modern ultra race – the challenge was one that put distance first. The speculation before the first Tour de France was not about who would win, or how fast they'd go, but simply if the whole ludicrous enterprise was even possible. Henri Desgrange, the man who was credited with devising the race, was deeply uncertain about what was going to happen when the first race set off from Paris. Most neutral observers were very sceptical about there being any finishers at all – and that was largely the point of the event. For the riders it was first and foremost an adventure, or maybe, given the professional nature of most of the early riders, more like a quest. There was a lot they didn't know, about the course, about their rivals, about themselves. An early race had a narrative that was only partly about results – I bet you know more stories from the early Tours de France than you know winners. A modern Tour rider doesn't often nurse themselves from village to village, wondering when the stage will end, wondering where they'll sleep if they ever make it. Their bike-racing ancestors did, and ultra riders still do. Now I feel like I know at least a little bit of what that's like.

There's no easy ultra race. No long race is ever truly under control, there's no such thing as having mastered it. Chris Murray was key to getting me back on my bike in the middle of the night at my second 24-hour. She's a previous three-time national champion and a British record holder, hugely experienced, a Lieutenant Colonel in the British Army, and one of the most effective bike riders I know. She went on to ride the 24-hour Worlds in California later the same year. At the Worlds she finished third, but only after some middle-of-the-night vomiting and what she described as 'a Hutch moment', when she got back to her team with firm plans to stop and go home and not to host a discussion about the issue. As she had not long before done for me, she was gently put back on her bike and sent back into the race.

The 'Hutch moment' isn't the sort of immortality I might have dreamed of, but I admit it made me feel part of something. These races have been a way to connect with some of the best cyclists I've ever met. They're very largely amateurs – the most that the majority of them might get from a sponsor would be a bit of a discount. But they're determined to find out what they're capable of, and how they cope with what the race brings. They wouldn't get involved if they didn't get something extraordinary out of it, and to do that I think they have to be a little bit extraordinary themselves.

I've had so much help and support from people who wanted nothing in return and were just keen to share their experience. People gave up weekends of their lives, summer weekends that they could have spent doing objectively more rewarding things. They exchanged them for dark nights, in lashing rain, sinking quietly into the mud of an A-road verge while they helped a not-obviously-grateful almost-stranger see what he might be able to do. They said that they enjoyed it. I don't know which worries me more: the strong likelihood that they didn't or the possibility that they really did.

I had the satisfaction of going back and picking up from that long-distant 'good' 12-hour race, and settling for myself that it wasn't just luck. I do indeed have the ability to ride a long race without it inevitably becoming a reenactment of the Battle of Waterloo. I can calmly and rationally work out what I should be able to do, make an appropriate plan, and then make a reasonable attempt to implement it. When I put it that way it doesn't sound like playing the Pyramid Stage at Glastonbury, but it's not supposed to. It's personal, it's small, that's why it was worth doing in the first place.

Not all of it went perfectly, but I don't think it ever does. Every long race is a bit of a saga, whoever you are. I didn't always ride as well as I could have. There are parts of my races that I look back at and wish I'd been more disciplined, or where I wish I'd made better choices – in my first 24 I'd have gone further if I'd dropped the effort level when things started to hurt because then I'd have been able to hold a

THE HUTCH MOMENT

better aerodynamic position in the late stages, and I'd have been able to eat better, and ride harder later. It's the terrible flow chart again, and like most flow charts, if you're in the middle of it it's just a maze. You learn, and a key skill for long races is how fast you learn and how many times you need to be told.

I learned that I can still push myself pretty hard. I'd wondered whether, in the years since I stopped racing seriously, I might have lost some competitive instinct. A friend of mine, who retired long before I did after a vastly more successful career, described himself to me as 'a recovering sportsman', and said he had no idea what sort of motivation could have pushed him to do the things he once did, make the sacrifices he once made. It turns out I haven't changed all that much.

I'd love to say, 'I found my limits', but I'm not sure there's really any such thing as a definitive limit. I'd have said I gave all I had in my first 24-hour race, but I also know that if halfway through someone had offered me an Olympic gold medal if I could wring out another 10 miles, I could have done it. I think there's a sort of demand and supply thing going on with this kind of race – what you can do is located at the intersection of the motivation you need and the motivation you have to do it. I know I gave it everything I could find at the time.

The lowest point of my 24-hour races was the three in the morning meltdown in 2024. There are two things about it. The first is that it pushed out the envelope a little for me. I'd had many, many conversations with athletes about 'bad patches', how you get through them, how you recover. There's Ian Walker's phrase about the need to believe that however bad things are they will always get better. I thought I'd experienced that sort of thing in previous races. I'd no idea just how bad it can get yet be recoverable. I probably ought to work the whole thing up into a motivational speech.

I've had a lot of fun. Really, I have. No one believes me when I tell them this because it goes against their expectations. I understand why most accounts of a long race have a distinct air of the misery-memoir about them, because it's box office. Cycling, more than any other sport or activity, prizes 'suffering'. It's the only activity where someone (the someone in this instance being a former colleague of mine) will complain that they paid £2,000 for a luxury holiday and didn't suffer as much as they expected to because the tour organizer mollycoddled them. Endurance cycling is supposed to make you unhappy. That's why people like it so much.

So no one wants to hear that you rode the Race Across America and it was 'fine', any more than they want to listen to a Tour de France winner saying it was 'simple'. Even if it was truly fine, it's only going to have been fine in the fairly specific context of ultra racing. If all you do is stick to the simple events of the race, you'll still be telling people about things they really don't like the sound of and they'll do the rest for you. Tell someone about chundering over your own feet in the pissing rain at three in the morning and they'll leap to the conclusion that this was a bad thing which would make for an unhappy time. And fair enough, in that moment things don't necessarily feel that great. (Ironically,

THE HUTCH MOMENT

if you do the same thing on an evening out everyone will assume you were having the night of your life.)

Those moments matter very much for another reason. The difficult parts of a race have a significant role in determining the result. You need to have a way to get through them. Knowing that other people have managed to survive sickness and exhaustion will help. An ultra rider who tells you about a night from hell might put you off the whole idea of an ultra race, or they might just as easily help you get through one. Mike Broadwith's 'Can you not do 20 minutes?' story is an important lesson, wrapped up in a tale of despair.

But it all means we don't pay enough attention to the wonderful bits. The parts of the race where it's going brilliantly, where despite the difficulty of what you're trying to do, you've everything in balance and you're eating up the miles by just tapping on the pedals. Riding through a dawn, having ridden all night, feeling the heat of the sun and seeing the mist in the hollows start to disappear. The experience of being part of a race where so many people are doing so many things. The straightforward sense of achieving something. Being part of a community that's devoted to doing something for the sheer love of it. The hard bits are how you earn the good bits, and the hard miles are what make the good miles sing.

Acknowledgements

A lot of people helped me with both my riding and my writing in the world of ultra racing, and I was often taken aback by their generosity with both time and support. As something of an outsider to long races, I wasn't sure what sort of reception I might get from some of the old hands when I arrived on their turf, but they could not have been more welcoming.

In particular, I must thank Mike Broadwith, who guided me through my own races, acting as both mentor and crew chief. I might have managed to start two 24-hour Championships without him, but I'm not convinced I'd have finished either of them.

My other helpers at the 24-hour races were Chris Murray, Paul Lewis, Julia Shaw, Andrew Watts, Tom Broadwith, Tim Bayley, Chris and Jane Brooks, and my partner Louisa. My Arctic Aircon teammates were Joe Gorman, Neil Lauder, Steve Abraham and Nick Clarke. Pete Ruffhead sponsors the team and has been a supporter of long distance racing and record breaking for many, many years. The 24-hour events I rode were organized by the Williams family and the Mersey Roads Club, who have for many years kept the wonderful event alive as the last remaining 24-hour race in the UK.

Athletes who shared their experiences of ultra races included Christoph Strasser, Fiona Kolbinger, Shu Pillinger, James Hayden, Rory Kemper, Leigh Timmis, Mark Turner, Ian Walker and especially Emily Chappell, who also took the time to introduce me to several other riders.

Other experts in various fields who were kind enough to help me included Bianca Broadbent, Josephine Perry, Charlotte Elsworth-Edelsten, Jamie Pringle, Mark Burnley, Jon Baker, Greg Whyte, Wendy Martinson, Roger Sparrow at Exposure Lights and chef Alan Murchison, whose several excellent books on food for athletes I'm very happy to recommend. The Race Across America organization let me sit in on several of the seminars they run for registered riders and teams.

I am deeply indebted to Charlotte Atyeo at Greyhound Literary.

And finally, my thanks to my excellent editor at Allen & Unwin, Ed Faulkner.

Index

accelerometers, 169–70
adaptation, 93–4, 96, 98, 99
addiction, 52
adenosine triphosphate (ATP), 62–5, 67, 94–5, 123
aero bars, 190, 191, 196, 199
aero helmets, 201
aerobic reactions, 63, 64–5, 94, 96–7, 121, 126, 128, 238
aerodynamics, 7, 25, 94, 140, 189–98, 237, 243
   body position and, 25, 56, 94, 190–98, 199, 200, 221, 222, 235, 249
Agricultural Hall, Islington, 81
Alavoine, Jean, 84
Aldi, 230
Alt Tour, 161
altitude, 93, 98, 99
amateur ethos, 19, 50, 102, 106, 152–3, 159, 160–65, 230
anaerobic reactions, 63, 64–5, 94
Anfield Bicycle Club, 213
anticipatory regulation, 32, 34
anxiety, 181
Appalachian mountains, 225

athlete's heart, 96
Atkins, Edith, 153
Australia, 9, 151, 158, 161, 228–9
L'Auto, 85

Baker, Jon, 139, 143
Barclay, Robert, 80
Bath, Somerset, 78
Bayley, Tim, 25–6
bereavement, 52
bicycles, 61, 187–8
   aero bars, 190, 191, 196, 199
   climbing bikes, 163, 225
   gears, 201–2
   road bikes, 190, 199, 200, 201
   saddles, 111, 189, 190, 192–5
   theft of, 187–8, 204
   time trial bikes, 190–92, 198, 200, 201
Biggleswade, Bedfordshire, 1
biochemistry, 31, 38, 62, 94, 237
   ATP, 62–5, 67, 94–5, 123
   lactate, 63–75, 88, 96, 100–101, 109, 110
Birmingham University, 193
Blackwell, H., 28

Blair Atholl, Perthshire, 120
blood, 31, 38, 62, 66, 95, 96, 99
  carbohydrate and, 124
  heat conditioning and, 115
Bob Graham Round, 138
body position, 11, 25, 109, 111, 237
  aerodynamics and, 25, 56, 94, 190–98, 199, 200, 221, 222, 235, 249
  digestion and, 140
body temperature, 32, 73, 115
Bol d'Or, 151
'bonk', 104
Bordeaux–Paris race, 119, 148
border posts, 228
Borg scale, 37
Bosoni, Victor, 234
brain, 30–34, 38, 43
  carbohydrate and, 124
  threat responses, 43, 48
brakes, 202–3
Brenner pass, 234
Brest, France, 159
Brighton, East Sussex, 29, 78
British Best All-Rounder, 18–19
Broadbent, Bianca, 192–5
Broadwith, Mike, 20, 24–8, 40, 47, 85, 87–8, 91, 108–9, 220, 251
  aerodynamics, 197–8
  commuting, 102
  electronics and, 206
  End-to-End record, 24, 68
  nutrition and, 133
  Shermer's Neck, 198
  sleep and, 172
  stopping and, 58, 172

Bryne, Richard, 199
Burnley, Mark, 72, 74, 104
Bury St Edmunds, Suffolk, 79
Butler, Gethin, 26, 29, 154

cable gears, 201
cadence, 89
caffeine, 168, 170, 180, 182–3
Cairngorms, 120
California, United States, 155, 156, 224, 247
calories, 121–2, 132, 138, 139, 140, 142, 230
Canada, 157
Cape Wrath, Highland, 149
carbohydrate, 3, 13, 32, 59, 63, 67, 95, 104, 123, 124–41
carbon emissions, 245–6
Carline, Nim, 70–71
catheters, 87–8
central governor theory, 31–4, 37, 38
central nervous system, 30–31, 34
Century Ride, 155–6
chains, 151, 203, 205, 234
Chamberlain, Neville, 151–2
Chappell, Emily, 56–8, 103, 143, 185
charity, 52, 226
Children in Need, 57
Christoph, Eugene, 84
circadian rhythm, 170–71, 184
climbing bikes, 163, 200, 225
climbs, 98, 40, 85, 88, 98, 107, 129, 182, 189, 225
  Everesting, 10
  hill-climb championships, 7

INDEX

clothing, 47, 91, 192, 196, 201, 205, 219
Coker, Amanda, 10
cold, 196, 219–22
colour coding, 86
colours game, 36–7
Commonwealth Games, 114
community, 16, 53, 54
commuting, 102–3
computers, 46–8, 89–90
Comrades Marathon, 32–3
conscious stopping, 37
Cornwall, England, 29, 68, 214
Coupe, Mick, 179–80
Cromack, Roy, 68–9
Cycling, 119
Cycling Time Trials (CTT), 30
Czechia, 231–2

deep resting, 170
Delhi Commonwealth Games (2010), 114
depression, 52
derny bicycles, 148
Desgrange, Henri, 82–4, 85, 246
Devon, England, 29, 68
doping, 99, 129, 162, 182
dot watching, 11, 16, 53, 160, 227, 233
down jackets, 204
dynamos, 207, 211, 226

eating, *see* food and drink
Edge, T.A., 213–15
Edinburgh–London, 9, 29, 150, 152
EF Education–EasyPost team, 161
EF Education–Nippo team, 9

effort level, 37
elbow-rest aero bars, 199
ElbSpitze, 107
electrolyte tablets, 205–6
electronic gears, 201–2
electronics, 46–8, 89–90, 206–8
Elliot, Jim, 199
Elsworth-Edelsten, Charlotte, 169–72, 175, 176, 179–81, 183
Ely, Cambridgeshire, 209
emotions, 58–9
Empire State Building, New York, 156
End-to-End, 9, 20, 24–8, 58, 161
    Broadwith's record, 24, 68
    Coupe's record, 179
    Edge's record, 213–15
    Fletcher's record, 215
    sleep and, 171–2, 179, 182
    Wilson's record, 151–3
    Woodburn's record, 119–21, 138, 179
Endure (Hutchinson), 33, 34
energy drinks, 3, 87, 99, 128, 130, 132, 134–5
energy gels, 3, 40, 43, 56, 128, 130, 133–4, 206
entry fees, 216
enzymes, 67, 95
epilepsy, 33
EPO (erythropoietin), 99, 129
equilibrium, 32, 93
equipment, 188–211
    aero bars, 190, 191, 196, 199
    bags, 188, 200, 204
    brakes, 202–3
    clothing, 47, 91, 192, 196, 201, 205, 219

equipment *(cont.)*
   electronics, 46–8, 89–90, 206–8
   gears, 201–2
   helmets, 91, 102, 191, 192, 198, 201
   lights, 208–11
   locks, 204
   shoes, 195, 204
   spare parts, 203, 205, 224
European North-to-South record, 200
European West-to-East record, 44, 175
Evenepoel, Remco, 197
Everesting, 10
excitement, 39
experience, 42
Exposure Lights, 209
eyebrow muscles, 94

Faster (Hutchinson), 35, 158
Fastest Known Time (FKT), 164
fat, 63, 67, 76, 94, 95, 100, 103–4, 122, 123–4
fatigue, 31–2, 36–8, 64, 68, 74, 100
flavour fatigue, 136–7
Fletcher, L., 215
Florida, United States, 157
flow charts, 238–9, 241, 249
follow vehicles, 44, 223–5
food and drink, 3, 6, 11, 13, 42, 59, 86–7, 119–45, 244
   body position and, 140
   calories, 121–2, 132, 138, 139, 140, 142
   carbohydrate, 3, 13, 32, 59, 63, 67, 95, 104, 123, 124–41

   colour coding, 86
   energy gels, 3, 40, 43, 56, 128, 130, 133–4, 206
   flavour fatigue, 136–7
   gas stations, 43, 56, 60, 133, 142, 206, 230–31
   gastrointestinal issues, 6, 220
   hydration, 67, 75, 87, 99, 116, 141, 143–4
   liquid strategy, 135–6, 220
   luggage and, 205–6
   mouth pain and, 140–41
   nutrition plans, 86, 109–10, 112, 120, 129–45
   oesophageal swelling and, 140
   sodium, 144–5
   solid foods, 130, 134–5
   unsupported events and, 141–2, 167
foot racing, 79–81
Fremantle–Sydney, 151
fructose, 128
fuel, 103–5, 110
   carbohydrate, 3, 13, 32, 59, 63, 67, 95, 104, 123, 124–45
   economy, 62, 100, 103, 121
   fat burning, 63, 67, 76, 94, 95, 100, 103–4, 122, 123–4
   metabolism and, 76, 121, 123
   protein, 104
functional threshold power (FTP), 65–6, 105, 106

G-forces, 75
gambling, 19, 81
Garin, Maurice, 83
gas stations, 43, 56, 60, 133, 142, 206, 230–31

INDEX

gastrointestinal issues, 6, 220
GBDURO, 161
gears, 201–2
gels, 3, 40, 43, 56, 128, 130, 133, 134
Gemperle, Robin, 176
Georgia, United States, 156
glucose syrup, 120–21
glycogen, 32
go-as-you-please racing, 80–81
Godwin, Tommy, 10
Golden Book of Cycling, The, 152
Google Street View, 11, 40, 160, 228, 242
Gore-Tex, 196
governing bodies, 30, 54, 81, 163, 164, 189
GPS, 70, 157, 164, 176, 207, 227, 230
Grant, Ulysses S., 224
gravel, 8, 9, 84, 158, 176, 177, 184, 189
Great Divide trail, 157
Grossglockner pass, 234
GSK, 141
Guinness World Record, 163, 189

haemoglobin, 99
Haldeman, Lon, 156
Hall, Mike, 157–8
hallucinations, 50, 104, 153, 168, 170, 177–9
Hartman, C.A., 28
Hayden, James, 198, 227
heart rate, 15, 68, 73, 75–6, 89, 90, 96, 124
heat conditioning, 32, 114–16
heat stress, 75–6

heel-and-toe walking, 79–80
helmets, 91, 102, 191, 192, 198, 201
Hercules, 151, 152
Highlands, Scotland, 68
highways, 228
hills, *see* climbs
Holland, Charles, 203
Holt, Harold, 151
homeostasis, 32, 93
hormones, 99
hot foot, 195
Houa, Léon, 82
Hour, The (Hutchinson), 35
Hutchinson, Alex, 33, 34
Hyde Park, London, 78
hydration, 67, 75, 87, 99, 116, 141, 143–4
hydraulic disc brakes, 202
hydrogel, 128
hyperthermia, 115
hypothermia, 196, 219–22

inclinometers, 111
Indian Pacific Wheel Race, 158
interconnectedness, 238, 240
interval training, 64, 106, 113
Ironman, 144, 182

jackets, 196, 204

K2 canoeing, 154
Kansas, United States, 199–200, 224
Kemper, Rory, 159, 161, 164
ketones, 124–6
Kolbinger, Fiona, 49, 52, 109, 142, 230, 239, 245

259

Kolbinger, Fiona *(cont.)*
   Transcontinental Race, 49, 106–7, 159, 231–2
Kyle of Durness, 149

lactate, 63–75, 88
   nutrition and, 123, 126–7
   training and, 96, 100–101, 109, 110, 114
Lambot, Firmin, 84
Land's End–John O'Groats, *see* End-to-End
Land's End–London, 29
last hour, 57
leapfrogging, 223
Lidl, 230
Liège–Bastogne–Liège, 82
lights, 208–11
liquid-only nutrition, 135–6, 220
Lisbon, Portugal, 44
Littlewood, George, 80–81
Liverpool–London, 9, 29, 78
logistics, 19, 20, 43–5
London, England, 77–8
   Olympic Games (2012), 125
London–Bath–London, 152
London–Brighton, 29
London–Edinburgh–London, 150
London–Edinburgh, 29, 152
London–Liverpool, 9, 29, 78, 152
London–Portsmouth–London, 152
Long Distance Championship, 81
Lost Dot, 159, 161
Lotus, 192
luggage, 188, 204

Mackenzie, Christina, 165, 172
Madison Square Garden, New York, 81–2
major highways, 228
Mallory, George, 50
maltodextrin, 128
Manchester Velodrome, 35
mantras, 45–6, 241
marathons, 34, 64, 89, 144
Marcora, Samuele, 36–7
Marin, 155
Marino, John, 156
Maryland, United States, 157
mass-start road races, 7, 8
mathematics, 132
Maurten, 128
meditation, 52, 174
mental fatigue, 36–8
Menzies, Robert, 151
Mercedes Sprinter, 224
Mersey Roads course, 208, 210
metabolism, 76, 121, 123
Mexico, 157
mitochondria, 95
mood swings, 58–9
Moore, James, 79
Morton, Lachlan, 9, 161, 229
motivation, 2, 37, 49–55, 245
mottos, 45–6, 241
mountain biking, 9, 155, 157
Mountains-to-Sea trail, 33, 34
mouth pain, 140–41
multi-day races, 49
Murchison, Alan, 130, 132–3
Murray, Chris, 135, 220–22, 247
muscles, 31–2, 38, 62–5, 67, 114
   ATP, 62–5, 67, 94–5, 123
   damage to, 73–4

interval training and, 113–14
sleep and, 171
Myall, John, 78

National 12 Hour Championship, 1–6, 8, 12–16, 53, 137, 243
National 24 Hour Championship, 25, 30, 54–5, 68, 97, 122, 163
   2023: 19–21, 23, 46–9, 85–92, 108–17, 128, 130, 133, 168, 209
   2024: 131, 209, 219, 247, 249–50
'nearly there', 55–7
neck muscles, 198
nerves, 39, 240
never-exceed effort level, 67, 68
New Jersey, United States, 157
New York, United States, 81, 156
Newmarket Heath, Suffolk, 80
nighttime riding, 40, 82, 83, 86–7, 90, 110, 208
Noakes, Tim, 31–3, 37
non-physical stress, 35–6
North Coast 500 circuit, 164–5
North Road Cycling Club, 208
North-to-South Europe record, 200
nutrition, 3, 6, 11, 13, 42, 59, 86–7, 109–10, 112, 119–45, 238, 244
   body position and, 140
   calories, 121–2, 132, 138, 139, 140, 142, 230
   carbohydrate, 3, 13, 32, 59, 63, 67, 95, 104, 123, 124–41
   energy gels, 3, 40, 43, 56, 128, 130, 133–4
   gas stations, 43, 56, 60, 133, 142, 206, 230–31
   gastrointestinal issues, 6, 220
   liquid strategy, 135–6, 220
   mouth pain and, 140–41
   nutritionists, 129, 141, 217
   sodium, 144–5
   unsupported events and, 141–2, 167
nutritionists, 129, 141, 217

oesophageal swelling, 140
Olympic Games, 24, 27, 125, 158
Opperman, Hubert, 150–51, 153
Oregon, United States, 156
oxygen, 31, 62–3, 67, 71–2, 73–4, 95, 96, 99

pacing, 37, 70, 90
Pan-Celtic Race, 158
Paris, France, 77
Paris–Brest–Paris, 149, 150
Paris–Roubaix, 82
Paris–Rouen, 79
pedestrianism, 79–80
Pelissier, Francis, 119
Pennine Way, 138
Perry, Josephine, 43, 48, 52, 55, 216, 219
Perth, Scotland, 24, 25, 119–20
physiology, 7, 12, 16, 17, 38, 61–77, 238
   ATP, 62–5, 67, 94–5, 123
   heart rate, 15, 68, 73, 75–6, 89, 90, 96, 124

physiology *(cont.)*
  lactate, 63–75, 88, 96, 100–101, 109, 110
  power output, 76, 89, 90, 114 121
Pillinger, Shu, 140–41
  Race Across America, 60, 137, 141, 177, 178–9, 225
  Transcontinental Race, 142–3, 177, 206–7
place-to-place records, 9–10, 28–30, 44, 78, 102, 119, 150–53, 164
  End-to-End, 20, 24, 26, 27–9, 66, 68, 150–53, 179
  European North-to-South, 200
  European West-to-East, 44, 175
planning
  route planning, 227–30
  scenario planning, 41–9, 240–43
plasma volume, 95
Poland, 229
Poole, Dick, 29
positive feedback loops, 39
Post Office, 79
potassium, 65
potholes, 113, 197, 208, 210
power banks, 207
power naps, 170–74
power output, 76, 89, 90, 114, 121
pre-race arousal, 39, 240
Pringle, Jamie, 12, 116
professional racing, 8, 36, 44, 147, 151, 160–64
protein, 104
ProTour, 8

psychology, 31, 38–60, 238–43
  mantras, 45–6, 241
  motivation, 2, 37, 49–55, 245
  planning, 41–9, 240–43
  pre-race arousal, 39, 240
  visualization exercises, 39–41, 240–41
psychomotor vigilance tests, 170
public tracking, 11, 16, 53, 160, 227, 233
punctures, 41, 84, 113, 167, 176, 206, 233, 234, 235

Race Across America, 10, 11, 17, 25, 156–7, 223–4, 250
  Elliot, 199
  equipment and, 189, 211
  heat and, 114
  neck braces, 198
  Pillinger, 60, 137, 141, 177, 178–9, 225
  power output study, 76
  Shermer, 198
  sleep and, 173, 174, 184
  Strasser, 42, 136, 173, 226
  support teams, 215–16, 217, 222, 223–4
  Whyte, 57, 58
  world records and, 163
Race Around Ireland, 9
Randonnée events, 149
records, 7, 9–10, 19, 28–30, 44, 49, 150–53
  Fastest Known Time, 164–5
  place-to-place, *see* place-to-place records
  24-hour, 30, 72–3, 74–5, 108, 139, 189

INDEX

world hour, 35
relaxation, 39
Repack races, 155
rim brakes, 202
road bikes, 190, 199, 200, 201
road helmets, 201
Road Records Association (RRA), 30, 164–5
Rocky Mountains, 157, 225
Romania, 229
Round the World record, 10
route planning, 227–30
Rowell, Charles, 81
Ruffhead, Pete, 25
Runner's World, 34
running, 169–70
Russia, 44
RVs, 44, 159, 175, 216, 224–5

saddles, 111, 189, 190, 192–5
San Diego, California, 163, 210
Santa Monica, California, 156
scenario planning, 41–9, 240–41
schedules, 26, 28, 68–70
Scunthorpe, Lincolnshire, 17
self-esteem, 52
Sheffield, South Yorkshire, 80–81
Sheridan, Eileen, 152–4
Shermer, Michael, 198
Shermer's Neck, 198, 201
Shimano, 203
Shiv bicycles, 61
shoes, 195, 204
short distance races, 39–40, 61–2
short-term goals, 55–6
Shropshire, England, 20, 48, 85, 115

Siddeley, John Davenport, 213–15
Sinyard, Mike, 155
six-day races, 80–81
six-hour rides, 110–11
skinsuits, 47, 91, 192, 201
sleep, 167–85
    caffeine and, 168, 170, 180, 182–3
    deprivation, 168, 170, 177–80, 183
    duration of, 173–7
    hallucinations and, 168, 170, 177–9
    issues with, 181
    luggage and, 204, 205
    periodization, 181–2
    power naps, 170–74
    unsupported events, 231–2
slogans, 45–6, 241
social media, 9, 44, 52, 160, 162
Southall, Frank, 153
spare parts, 203, 205, 224
Specialized, 61, 155
Spine Race, 138, 172–3, 178
sponsorship, 7, 8–9, 12, 15, 44, 83, 85, 147, 165, 218, 226
    amateur ethos and, 230
    equipment provision, 129, 218
SRAM, 203
Stansted Airport, Essex, 208–9
Stanton, David, 81
stopping, 3–4, 5, 25, 37, 43, 57–8, 172–3
Strasser, Christoph, 42, 50, 74, 91, 105–6, 107, 109, 226, 239
    comfort, views on, 190, 196, 197

Strasser, Christoph *(cont.)*
　equipment, 189, 205
　nutrition plans, 128, 136, 139, 142
　route planning, 229
　sleep, 173–4
　wrong way riding, 227
Strava, 164, 228
stress, 35–6, 181
Strong, Pauline, 154
sunk cost fallacy, 55
support teams, 3, 4, 14, 19, 20, 40, 42, 44–5, 53, 60, 157, 159, 213–26
　conflicts, 216–17
　follow vehicles, 44, 223–5
　leapfrogging, 223
　lights and, 210–11
　'nearly there' and, 57
　nutrition and, 86, 141, 142, 143, 217, 220
　sleep and, 177, 184, 220
　trust, 219, 221, 222
sweating, 144

Taylor, John, 70
Taylor, Lynne, 153, 154
temperature, 32, 114–16
thinking, 38–9
threat responses, 43, 48
time, perception of, 33–4, 47–8, 56–7
time trial bikes, 190–92, 198
time trial position, 190
timekeepers, 2, 29, 68
Timmis, Leigh, 44–6, 175, 184
Tour de France, 9, 24, 82–5, 97, 147, 150, 158, 160, 207, 246–7

aero bar revolution, 200
Holland and, 203
training for, 98
VO2 max and, 71
Tour Divide, 157
training, 93–117
　adaptation, 93–4, 96, 98, 99
　commuting as, 102–3
　consistency, 99
　heat conditioning, 32, 114–16
　interval training, 64, 106, 113
　nighttime riding, 110
　nutrition plans, 109–10, 112
　specificity, 98–101
Transcontinental Race (TCR), 9, 10, 53, 56, 84, 151, 158, 159–60
Bosoni, 234
Broadwith, 206
Chappell, 103
equipment and, 188, 189, 211
gravel parcours, 84, 176, 227
Hayden, 198
Kolbinger, 49, 106–7, 159, 231–2
Pillinger, 142–3, 177, 206–7
pre-race coverage, 188, 203–4
sleep and, 176–7, 184
Strasser, 42, 176, 189, 226, 227
Timmis, 184
Walker, 102
trucks, 229
Turner, Elizabeth, 79
Turner, Mark, 138, 172–3, 178
24 Hour Fellowship, 97
24 Hour Story, The (Taylor), 70

INDEX

24-hour track record, 30, 72–3, 74–5, 108, 139, 189
tyres, 82, 202, 203, 205, 206, 233, 244

UCI (Union Cycliste Internationale), 8, 148
Ultra Trail de Mont Blanc (UTMB), 169, 171
Ulysses, Kansas, 224
United States, 154–7
unsupported events, 9, 19, 34, 42, 53, 84, 107, 157–8, 159, 226–35
   lights and, 210
   nutrition and, 141–2, 167, 230–31
   public tracking, 11, 16, 53, 160, 227, 233
   route planning, 227–30
   sleep, 231–2
Ural mountains, 44

Van Deren, Diane, 33–4
Victorian era, 1, 19, 28, 77, 154, 163*n*, 164, 246
visualization exercises, 39–41, 240–41
VO2 max, 71–2, 74, 105

wagers, 19, 81
Walker, Ian, 102–3, 105, 200, 229, 250
walking, 79–81
Washington, DC, United States, 156
watch-keeping patterns, 175
wet wipes, 205
Where There's a Will (Chappell), 56, 57
Whyte, Greg, 57, 76–7
Wick, Caithness, 152, 214
Wide World of Sports, 156
Wilkinson, Andy, 29, 68–9
Wilson, Marguerite, 151, 153
wind tunnels, 190, 191, 192, 193, 196
women, 151–4, 172, 239–40
Woodburn, John, 24, 119–21, 138, 154
World 24-hour Championships, 163, 210, 247
World Bicycle Relief, 9
World Championships (UCI), 6
world hour record, 35
World Tour, 8, 66, 125, 129, 139, 160–61
World Ultra Cycling Association, 163*n*
Wrexham, Clwyd, 85, 91

York, North Yorkshire, 78
Yukon Arctic Ultra, 33

Žatec, Czechia, 231–2
Zwift, 113

About the Author

Michael Hutchinson is a writer, journalist and former professional cyclist. As a rider he won multiple national titles in both Britain and Ireland and competed at the World Championships and the Commonwealth Games.

As a writer, he wrote the award-winning *The Hour* about his attempt on cycling's most famous and sought-after record. He followed that up with *Faster*, about the training, the science, the genetics and the luck behind the world's fastest riders, and *Re:Cyclists*, a history of cyclists from 1816 to the present day.

He is a columnist for *Cycling Weekly* magazine, and his writing has appeared in the *Guardian*, *Observer*, *Financial Times*, *New York Times* and *New York Review of Books*, and he has presented cycling TV and radio shows for the BBC and others. Before he did any of that he was a legal academic at Cambridge and Sussex universities. He now lives with far too many bicycles in London and Cambridgeshire.